Strategic Management in Central and Eastern Europe

Strategic Management in Central and Eastern Europe has been co-published simultaneously as *Journal of East-West Business,* Volume 5, Number 4 1999.

The *Journal of East-West Business* Monographic "Separates"

Below is a list of "separates," which in serials librarianship means a special issue simultaneously published as a special journal issue or double-issue *and* as a "separate" hardbound monograph. (This is a format which we also call a "DocuSerial.")

"Separates" are published because specialized libraries or professionals may wish to purchase a specific thematic issue by itself in a format which can be separately cataloged and shelved, as opposed to purchasing the journal on an on-going basis. Faculty members may also more easily consider a "separate" for classroom adoption.

"Separates" are carefully classified separately with the major book jobbers so that the journal tie-in can be noted on new book order slips to avoid duplicate purchasing.

You may wish to visit Haworth's website at . . .

http://www.haworthpressinc.com

. . . to search our online catalog for complete tables of contents of these separates and related publications.

You may also call 1-800-HAWORTH (outside US/Canada: 607-722-5857), or Fax 1-800-895-0582 (outside US/Canada: 607-771-0012), or e-mail at:

getinfo@haworthpressinc.com

Strategic Management in Central and Eastern Europe, edited by Peter Geib, PhD, and Lucie Pfaff, PhD (Vol. 5, No. 4, 1999). *Containing thorough and extensive research, this valuable book will help you understand transition economies, conduct better business with them, and assist these countries in establishing profitable businesses.*

Marketing Challenges in Transition Economies of Europe, Baltic States and the C.I.S., edited by Gopalkrishnan R. Iyer, PhD, and Lance A. Masters, PhD (Vol. 5, No. 1/2, 1999). *"This book is a practical presentation of the problems that Central and Eastern Europe countries have had in changing from a command economy to a market economy. This book helps provide a much-needed analysis of why the good intentions of western governments and firms as well as transition economy governments and firms have not had more success in changing to a market economy." (James W. Littlefield, Professor of Marketing, Virginia Polytechnic Institute, Blacksburg, Virginia)*

Enterprise Restructuring and Foreign Investment in the Transforming East: The Impact of Privatization, edited by Val Samonis (Vol. 4, No. 1/2, 1998). *"This impressive volume represents a significant contribution to the rapidly growing literature on private sector development in transition economies." (Peter Cornelius, PhD, Chief International Economist, Deutsche Bank Research, Frankfurt, Germany)*

Marketing in Central and Eastern Europe, edited by Jan Nowak (Vol. 3, No. 1, 1997). *"Identify[ies] the methodological requirements for doing effective marketing research in the countries of Central and Eastern Europe." (Journal of Economic Literature)*

East-West Business Relationships: Establishment and Development, edited by Jarmo Nieminen (Vol. 1, No. 4, 1996). *"Recommended as first-rate reading for all those interested and involved in east-west business transactions and direct investment in eastern European countries." (Adam Gwiazda, PhD, Professor of International Economics, Gdansk University, Poland)*

The Central and Eastern European Markets: Guideline for New Business Ventures, edited by Petr Chadraba (Vol. 1, No. 3, 1995). *"An interesting collection of strategies and approaches to rapidly evolving markets in central and Eastern Europe." (George Tesar, PhD, Professor of Marketing, University of Wisconsin-Whitewater)*

Strategic Management in Central and Eastern Europe

Peter Geib
Lucie Pfaff
Editors

Strategic Management in Central and Eastern Europe has been co-published simultaneously as *Journal of East-West Business,* Volume 5, Number 4 1999.

International Business Press
An Imprint of
The Haworth Press, Inc.
New York • London • Oxford

Published by

International Business Press®, 10 Alice Street, Binghamton, NY 13904-1580 USA

International Business Press® is an imprint of The Haworth Press, Inc., 10 Alice Street, Binghamton, NY 13904-1580 USA.

Strategic Management in Central and Eastern Europe has been co-published simultaneously as *Journal of East-West Business,* Volume 5, Number 4 1999.

The development, preparation, and publication of this work has been undertaken with great care. However, the publisher, employees, editors, and agents of The Haworth Press and all imprints of The Haworth Press, Inc., including The Haworth Medical Press® and Pharmaceutical Products Press®, are not responsible for any errors contained herein or for consequences that may ensue from use of materials or information contained in this work. Opinions expressed by the author(s) are not necessarily those of The Haworth Press, Inc.

Cover design by Thomas J. Mayshock Jr.

Library of Congress Cataloging-in-Publication Data

Strategic management in Central and Eastern Europe / Peter Geib, Lucie Pfaff, editors.
     p. cm.
     "Strategic management in Central and Eastern Europe has been co-published simultaneously as Journal of East-West business, volume 5, number 4, 1999."
     Includes bibliographical references and index.
     ISBN 0-7890-0994-3 (alk. paper)–ISBN 0-7890-0995-1 (pbk : alk. paper)
     1. Strategic planning–Europe, Eastern. 2. Management–Europe, Eastern. I. Geib, Peter J. II. Pfaff, Lucie, 1929-
HD30.28 .S7322 2000
658.4$'$012$'$0943–dc21
                                                              00-022257

INDEXING & ABSTRACTING

Contributions to this publication are selectively indexed or abstracted in print, electronic, online, or CD-ROM version(s) of the reference tools and information services listed below. This list is current as of the copyright date of this publication. See the end of this section for additional notes.

- *BUBL Information Service, an Internet-based Information Service for the UK higher education community <URL: http://bubl.ac.uk/>*

- *Business & Management Practices*

- *CNPIEC Reference Guide: Chinese National Directory of Foreign Periodicals*

- *Contents Pages in Management (University of Manchester Business School), England*

- *FINDEX (www.publist.com)*

- *GEO Abstracts (GEO Abstracts/GEOBASE)*

- *Guide to Social Science & Religion*

- *Human Resources Abstracts (HRA)*

- *Index to Periodical Articles Related to Law*

- *Management & Marketing Abstracts*

- *Operations Research/Management Science*

- *Personnel Management Abstracts*

- *Political Science Abstracts*

- *Referativnyi Zhurnal (Abstracts Journal of the All-Russian Institute of Scientific and Technical Information)*

- *Social Services Abstracts*

- *Sociological Abstracts (SA)*

(continued)

*Special Bibliographic Notes related to special journal issues
(separates) and indexing/abstracting:*

- indexing/abstracting services in this list will also cover material in any "separate" that is co-published simultaneously with Haworth's special thematic journal issue or DocuSerial. Indexing/abstracting usually covers material at the article/chapter level.

- monographic co-editions are intended for either non-subscribers or libraries which intend to purchase a second copy for their circulating collections.

- monographic co-editions are reported to all jobbers/wholesalers/approval plans. The source journal is listed as the "series" to assist the prevention of duplicate purchasing in the same manner utilized for books-in-series.

- to facilitate user/access services all indexing/abstracting services are encouraged to utilize the co-indexing entry note indicated at the bottom of the first page of each article/chapter/contribution.

- this is intended to assist a library user of any reference tool (whether print, electronic, online, or CD-ROM) to locate the monographic version if the library has purchased this version but not a subscription to the source journal.

- individual articles/chapters in any Haworth publication are also available through the Haworth Document Delivery Service (HDDS).

Strategic Management
in Central and Eastern Europe

CONTENTS

ABOUT THE EDITORS

Peter Geib has earned a post-doctoral fellowship from Yale University in management and policy. He holds a PhD from the University of Michigan in political science and foreign policy. His dissertation focuses on trade policy formulation. Dr. Geib is Professor of international business and management and Coordinator of the International Business Program at Moorhead State University in Minnesota. He has conducted research on transition economies beginning with on-site interviews in China in 1988-1989. After the fall of the Berlin Wall he concentrated for several years on Central European economies. In the summers of 1991-1996 he conducted interviews in the Czech Republic, Poland, and Hungary. This research on transition economies and their strategic management implications has continued with efforts in Vietnam, Hong Kong, and Singapore, where Dr. Geib is currently on sabbatical.

Lucie Pfaff received a PhD from New York University in literature. Later changing fields by combining literature and economics, she earned her MA in economics and MBA in international business from Fairleigh Dickinson University, followed by a DBA in international marketing from International Graduate School. Dr. Pfaff became Coordinator of the International Business Program at the College of Mt. St. Vincent in 1982. She is presently Professor of business/economics at the College of Mt. St. Vincent, teaching courses in international economics and finance. Dr. Pfaff's research on Eastern Europe dates back to a Master's thesis entitled "Trade Relations Between Comecon and the European Community." Since then, she has been involved in research in comparative economics, trade and investment. In 1989 her focus shifted to studying the process of economic transformation from central command to market economy and the implications for Western companies in regard to strategic management in emerging markets.

Strategic Management
in Central and Eastern Europe:
Introduction

Peter Geib
Lucie Pfaff

The central European transition from planned economies to democratic capitalism is one of the most dramatic stories of the second half of the twentieth century. The process has many dimensions. The aim of this volume is to explore several business issues directly related to this process with a particular focus on issues relating to macro-economics and the cultural environment of international business. Business development in Poland, Hungary, and the Czech Republic has shown remarkable progress as these countries join NATO and prepare to join the European Union. Russia is an entirely different story as it struggles to find a fundamental economic and political identity. This volume provides an exploration of specific strategic management issues, but this edition is unique because it carefully examines context and the cultural environment. Moreover, these scholars look at a variety of functional issues including finance, strategy, human resources, and marketing.

Peter Geib is Professor of Management and Director of International Business at Moorhead State University, Moorhead, MN 56563.

Lucie Pfaff is Professor of Business/Economics and Coordinator of the International Business Program at the College of Mount Saint Vincent, Riverdale, NY 10471.

[Haworth co-indexing entry note]: "Strategic Management in Central and Eastern Europe: Introduction." Geib, Peter, and Lucie Pfaff. Co-published simultaneously in *Journal of East-West Business* (International Business Press, an imprint of The Haworth Press, Inc.) Vol. 5, No. 4, 1999, pp. 1-4; and: *Strategic Management in Central and Eastern Europe* (ed: Peter Geib, and Lucie Pfaff) International Business Press, an imprint of The Haworth Press, Inc., 2000, pp. 1-4. Single or multiple copies of this article are available for a fee from The Haworth Document Delivery Service [1-800-342-9678, 9:00 a.m. - 5:00 p.m. (EST). E-mail address: getinfo@haworthpressinc.com].

The paper by Zapalska and Zapalska provides important insights into the Hungarian transition. The authors seek to explain the role of entrepreneurship in the transformation. One important contribution is that the authors consider change on a variety of levels. The analysis shows how the emerging entrepreneurial economy fulfills important material and ideological functions. The authors assess Hungarian entrepreneurship within the context of macro-economic growth and the development of the banking system.

In addition to explaining the growth of small business ventures in terms of macroeconomic development and ideology, Zapalska and Zapalska also assess the idiosyncratic level of impact. The authors use survey data to show the relative importance of motivations and perceptions regarding entrepreneurial activity. Some of the variables examined include the desire for wealth, need for power, achievement, and career security. Moreover, the authors describe the problems associated with the lack of intellectual capital in Hungary such as training and education. This paper is clearly an important and sophisticated addition.

The paper by Sheila Puffer is a thorough examination of the cultural and ethical foundation of business development in Russia. Her paper underlines one of the significant realities of business and management, the underlying cultural core values. Russia is of course one of the most important case studies. Puffer shows the confusion in value change internally in Russia as well as the confusion that results from the culture clash as western countries seek to do business with Russia. Moreover, Puffer highlights emerging political and social institutions like the oligarchs and their influence on business.

Dawson and Henley provide us with an important sector case study in Poland's dynamic transition economy. They examine the internationalization of hypermarket retailing against the background of Poland's stunning advance. The authors provide an extensive analysis of macro-economic statistics and statistics relating to the retail network in Poland, the size distribution of stores and the number of firms by size of store network. The authors look at key factors such as staff development and the development of a service-orientated retail culture. Perhaps most importantly, the authors integrate their analysis with an explanation of the strategic implications of hypermarket development. These strategic implications include consideration of competitive factors, leveraging scale benefits, managing supply chains, logistics management, and the capital spending problems. The authors make it clear that becoming competitive means shaping systems to work effectively in the Polish context. The authors emphasize the ultimate importance of a market presence to establish first mover advantages.

Geib and Pfaff aim to explain the central European cultural environment on privatization and entry strategies. After decades of rigid central planning, the central European countries are in the midst of slow, painful, traumatic changes on their way to market economies. The geographic area focus is on Hungary, Poland, and the Czech Republic. The core of their research is based on data collection and interviews conducted by both authors between 1990 and 1998. The authors conducted more than 100 interviews over six years with managers in U.S. firms and joint ventures as well as focused research in Germany regarding the privatization process. The evidence is used to examine how cultural conditioning impacts on privatization and market entry strategies.

Geib and Pfaff examine changing political culture. In each case there is a rapid political change from authoritarian political culture to distinctly pluralistic democratic systems. Another important example of changing cultural context is the changing system of work-related social values. While collective values retain a strong hold, the cultural context increasingly emphasizes social and market-oriented values of individuality, initiative, risk, and profit. The authors also focus on privatization models and processes in each country, Poland, Hungary, and the Czech Republic. But many of the most important obstacles to progress stem from the legacy of communism–outmoded infrastructure, lack of a sound banking system, as well as the absence of a functional legal code. Finally, the authors describe entry strategies for the changing cultural environment.

Zapalska, Fogel, and Brozik examine one of the most important and intriguing questions, the credibility of the banking and financial management system. The authors focus on Hungary and Poland. The aim of their research is to describe the nature and level of competition in the banking sector in these two countries. Their research reveals considerable progress in establishing an independent commercial banking system since reforms started in the late 1980s. The authors first provide background regarding the banking sector in Hungary and Poland. Banking services in Hungary have undergone considerable development in recent years. It is clear that a good mix between Hungarian banks and foreign-owned banks has developed in Hungary. In Poland the main problem is restructuring away from the highly centralized traditional system as well as the neccssity of continued privatization.

In order to understand competitive forces in the banking sector, the authors conducted substantial survey research. In terms of competitive strategy, most bank managers seem to follow a long-term orientation of product innovation, the adoption of advanced technologies, a focus on market niche strategies, and improvement of quality standards and customer service operations. The authors evaluate these strategic orientations against the backdrop of more effective public macro-economic policy including deregulation and privatization. In their analysis the authors describe some of the most important policy debates such as the discussion over whether to adopt the American model, the German model, or the Japanese model.

Small Business Ventures
in Post-Communist Hungary

Alina Zapalska
Lucyna Zapalska

SUMMARY. Economic analysis on emerging economies of Central and Eastern Europe (CEE) has shown a flourishing private sector coexisting with shrinking state enterprises fueling speculation that growth would come from the new private sector. In this view, it is important to (1) assess the private sector which continues to grow and is vital to the process of emerging new market economies; and (2) account for the current place of entrepreneurship and assign its role in the process of systemic transformation which takes place in the economies of the CEE. Based on interviews and models on entrepreneurship, the paper analyzes how the entrepreneurs' behavior is influenced by government regulation, credit terms, taxation, long-term and short-term financing options, level of infrastructure, and preferences to small business, and how entrepreneurs' consequent behavior can in turn influence the working system itself. The goal is to show that the emerging small business sector of the post-Communist Hungarian economy fulfills important material and ideological functions. The paper concludes that the Hungarian entrepreneurship is an independent vehicle for economic growth and bringing about the emergence of capitalist forms of economic production in the post-Communist Hungarian economy. *[Article copies available for a fee from The Haworth Document Delivery Service: 1-800-342-9678. E-mail address: getinfo@ haworthpressinc.com <Website: http://www.haworthpressinc.com>]*

KEYWORDS. Hungary, business transition, entrepreneurship, entrepreneurial motivations, macro-economic growth

---

Alina Zapalska is Associate Professor of Economics at Marshall University, 400 Hal Greer Boulevard, Huntington, WV 25755.

Lucyna Zapalska is attorney at law, Rynek Glowny 44/13, Krakow 31-017, Poland.

[Haworth co-indexing entry note]: "Small Business Ventures in Post-Communist Hungary." Zapalska Alina, and Lucyna Zapalska. Co-published simultaneously in *Journal of East-West Business* (Internationa Business Press, an imprint of The Haworth Press, Inc.) Vol. 5, No. 4, 1999, pp. 5-21; and: *Strategi Management in Central and Eastern Europe* (ed: Peter Geib, and Lucie Pfaff) International Business Press an imprint of The Haworth Press, Inc., 2000 , pp. 5-21. Single or multiple copies of this article are availabl for a fee from The Haworth Document Delivery Service [1-800-342-9678, 9:00 a.m. - 5:00 p.m. (EST). E-mai address: getinfo@haworthpressinc.com].

INTRODUCTION

In order to revitalize the post-communist Hungarian economy through the creation of new business ventures it is important to understand the characteristics of entrepreneurs and the challenges they encounter. There is a growing consensus that the economic success for Central and Eastern Europe (CEE) will come from newly formed small and medium-sized enterprises. It is imperative to develop a more meaningful understanding of the characteristics and problems of small and medium-sized enterprises in CEE in order to help shape regional planning policy that would assist in small and medium-sized enterprise start-up, survival, and growth.

To that end, a survey was administered to identify primary causes of small business success and the types of problems encountered by those emerging entrepreneurial organizations. The study serves as a starting point for the conceptualization and systematic examination of entrepreneurial climate in post-Communist Hungary. The paper also provides implications for policy making that may be used by other countries of CEE in which the transition proceeds at a slower pace.

BACKGROUND

The year 1989 was a turning point for a number of countries in Central and Eastern Europe, in particular in Hungary, due to the decision to embark on a process of transformation to a full-fledged market economy. In contrast to other countries in the region, Hungary had come to the economic transformation with an already well-developed tradition of economic reforms. Those reforms of 1968 were intended to replace the economic system based on bureaucratic control with the so-called *New Economic Mechanism* (NEM) which encompassed the elimination of centrally determined plan targets, decentralization of some decision-making responsibilities to state-owned enterprises, acceptance of profit-oriented incentives schemes, institutional innovations, some market coordination, improved ability to compete in foreign markets by the substantial opening of the economy, and the development of some policy instruments and arrangements for carrying out indirect macroeconomic control through monetary and fiscal means. Although the private sector was encouraged by the reform, the

NEM constrained the increase of its share, and limited its activity to small-scale production and the service sector. The changes of 1968 were insufficient for establishing an efficient market system, even if there had been no powerful opposition to the reforms. Prices, profits, exchange rates, etc., have started to play an active role, but with severe distortions when compared with established market economies.

In the early 1980s, Hungary recognized the need for more radical economic reforms as well as the imperative of coupling them with political reforms. From the mid-1980s, the beginning of a new, more ambitious reform effort became apparent, and the political events of 1989 further broadened the scope of Hungarian economic transformation in the sense that Hungary would embrace private ownership and all the institutions of a market economy. Hungarian authorities have created a comprehensive legal framework to encourage the establishment of private enterprises as well as the transformation of state-owned enterprises and cooperatives into joint stock companies and other forms of business, especially with foreign participation. At the same time, the population learned to cope with falling real wages and searched for alternative income outside the public sector.

Under this new legal framework, there has been explosion in the number of new small private enterprises. Their dramatic growth, combined with the stagnation of state-owned enterprises, increased their portion of the economy. Most of those small firms in post-Communist Hungary are similar in many respects to small businesses that can be found in Western market economies. They have started to produce goods and services for local markets, become subcontractors of large state-owned enterprises, and created new jobs for the Hungarian labor market. Political stake holders of the old regime as well as black marketers made up a considerable portion of new entrepreneurs. The business success of those businesses allows them to raise enough credit in addition to their private capital to finance a major takeover. Some of the private firms arrived from the privatization and the formation of joint ventures with foreign participants. Hungary began attracting foreign investment earlier than other countries of CEE. Already in the 1970s Hungary passed legislation that allowed foreigners to control up to 49 percent of joint ventures, though foreign investment remained low. On January 1989, the Law on Nonresident Investment enabled foreigners to exercise 100 percent ownership. After that, foreign investment increased sharply. A number of key building-blocks of a market economy, such as a coherent tax system, a company law, and a two-tier banking system, were put in place. Table 1 presents a chronological list of antecedents to the establishment of small private entrepreneurial ventures.

Small privately owned firms are essential to the development of a competitive market economy in Eastern and Central Europe; there have been numerous positive consequences of their development in the Hungarian economy. First, their development substantially contributed to the creation of new jobs, stabilized the supply of essential consumer goods and services, increased the range of industrial production; and secondly, they have a substantial role in fostering the images of competitiveness, risk-taking, mobility, and other values essential to the successful functioning of an economic system that relies on market mechanism.

TABLE 1. Antecedents to the Establishment of Small Private Entrepreneurial Ventures

---

Six Antecedents to the establishment of private enterprises created an entrepreneurial climate in Hungary that has contributed to the success of Hungary's current economic transformation:

1960s-1970s: those working on state farms and agricultural cooperatives were allowed to use their household plots for more and more activities;

1970s-1980s: tenants were given opportunities to buy their state-owned apartments at between 15-30 percent of their market value;

1970s-1980s: auctions were used on large-scale farms to permit employees to bid for subcontracted responsibilities and in cities to distribute leases of restaurants and retail shops.

1970s-1980s: foreign participation as a minority partner in joint ventures was encouraged.

1980s: economic working teams were established in state-owned enterprises to allow entrepreneurs to establish small-scale centers. These teams were freed from many of the bureaucratic restrictions normally applied to enterprises and were able to offer "after work" for competitively determined wages.

1985: an amendment to the Act on State Enterprises transferred the ownership rights of 75 percent of enterprises to enterprise councils.

1986: the Law on Nonresident Investment enabled foreigners to exercise 100 percent ownership.

APPROACHES TO STUDYING ENTREPRENEURSHIP

In general, entrepreneurship is a multi-dimensional process and, hence, approaches to studying entrepreneurship focus on the characteristics, traits, and behavior of individual entrepreneurs, and socio, economic and political infrastructure that promotes or hampers the creation and development of entrepreneurship.

A number of scholars have suggested numerous factors that promote or hinder the emergence of entrepreneurship. According to economic literature, market incentives create entrepreneurial opportunities to be exploited, and capital is the major resource needed to carry out the entrepreneurial function (Schumpeter 1934, Kilby 1971, Jones et al. 1980, Tyson et al. 1994). Several scholars have developed theories and conducted studies that demonstrate the inseparability of the external environment from the entrepreneurial process (Hornaday et al. 1970, 1971, Kilby 1971, Sexton 1989, Stevenson 1985, Kent 1984, Gartner 1989a, 1989b). They consider the impact of monetary, fiscal and regulatory environments on entrepreneurial activity, and argue that in highly competitive environments, entrepreneurial ventures appear to promote high levels of innovation and firm performance.

An approach now gaining popularity explains entrepreneurship by combining economic variables with more personal, sociological variables and environmental influences (Gartner 1989a, 1989b). A variety of socio-cultural factors–legitimacy, social mobility, marginality, social integration, security, ideology, and other motives–have been proposed as influential for the appearance of successful entrepreneurship. Gartner (1989a, 1989b) explains entrepreneurs as those individuals who possess traits that cause them to seek out entrepreneurial opportunities to a greater extent than others. Over the years, numerous studies have supported various sets of personality characteristics of entrepreneurship: motivation, desire for wealth, need for control, power, opportunity, achievement, challenge, self-interest, vision of business ideas, risk-taking, and innovation. In sum, the traditional definitions are grouped into the following categories: entrepreneurship as innovation, entrepreneurship as risk-taking, entrepreneurship as stabilizing force, and entrepreneurship as founding, owning and managing a small business (Brockhouse 1987). The diversity of definitions that have been offered implies differences in policy choices (Tyson et al. 1994).

Based on the above approaches to entrepreneurship, the survey was developed to examine how the new small business owners' behavior is influenced by environmental conditions in the post-Communist economy and how the entrepreneurial behavior can, in turn, influence the working system itself. This is accomplished by (1) identifying barriers to small business development perceived by small business owners and operators; (2) examining environmental elements and factors of the entrepreneurial process; and (3) making an assessment of desirable changes for promoting greater entrepreneurial development in Hungary.

Entrepreneurial activity that results from the interaction of individual characteristics, turning points in individual lives, background, and cultural factors, and exposure to examples of success has been used in this paper to identify Hungarian entrepreneurship.

This paper also examines how the success of entrepreneurial talent depends on (1) macro-economic conditions including inflation, the competitive environment, and infrastructure; (2) government policies such as taxation, regulations, and preferences to small businesses; and (3) the financial environment, in particular the banking system.

It is hoped that this paper will enhance the understanding of small entrepreneurial organizations, and explain their current place and role in the process of transformation from a Communist economy to a market economy in Hungary.

SURVEY

This research study is based on a survey that was conducted in Hungary in 1994. Surveys were mailed to 125 entrepreneurs and followed up by telephone interviews to clarify certain items from the written surveys and to follow up with non-respondents. Interviews took place in the Hungarian language. The local Chamber of Commerce and the National Association of Entrepreneurs in Hungary provided assistance in contacting small business owners.

The primary questionnaire was based upon other studies with some modification (Zapalska 1997a, b and c). In order to understand and profile the entrepreneurs' problems and issues, the questionnaire elicited information about demographic and business characteristics; motivation for starting a business; entrepreneurial characteristics; primary cause of business; small business success; perceived difficulties in entrepreneurial development; and satisfaction with socio-economic conditions including government regulations, credit terms, taxation, long-term and short-term financing options, and representation of and preferences to small businesses.

RESULTS

The first section of the survey asked respondents to provide demographic information including age, education, knowledge, location, family background, experience, and psychological characteristics. According to the results, the majority of respondents are between 35 and 55 years of age. Education played an important role in the background of Hungarian small business owners. The sample was spread among high school, college and university level. Nearly 45 percent of respondents had a college degree and about 88 percent of respondents indicated a middle or upper-class environment. Respondents demonstrated a propensity to take risk, an urge for excellence, a desire to be independent, and a readiness for change whenever the competitive market situation forced them to do so in order to grow and survive. They also seemed to possess social skills such as persuasiveness, low need for support, goal setting, commitment to work, self-confidence, low conformity and lack of emotionalism. All these characteristics enhanced the entrepreneurs' propensities to start a business. Many expressed that their abilities, skills and education have been essential for their success and struggle with the difficulties of operating their businesses in uncertain and difficult conditions of the economic transformation. The entrepreneurs expressed that the comparatively high overall level of education of the labor force is clearly a major advantage as it facilitates on-the-job skill formation. The majority of respondents had gained experience from their previous operations or work for the state-owned enterprise. They have been working for extended periods of time.

Using Brockhouse's (1987) approach, we asked our respondents to identify which of "the roles of entrepreneurship" they could identify themselves. The majority of respondents stated that their business involved innovation via development of new products, sources, new methods of production, creation of new markets, new sources of supply and development of new organizational forms and managerial techniques. They also expressed that they clearly placed their capital at a high degree of risk and promoted very risky projects. All of them run, own, and manage their businesses and see themselves as a stabilizing force in the national economy. The small business owners were asked to specify the nature of the businesses and their size, measured by number of employees. The results are presented in Table 2 and Table 3, respectively.

The type of business venture varied widely from the very innovative to traditional areas like services, manufacturing, or retailing. About 36 percent of Hungarian businesses were engaged in small-scale manufacturing. Service activities accounted for about 64 percent. Some businesses were based on product innovation or product modification, creation of new markets, methods of production and

TABLE 2. Nature of Small Business Venture

Type of Business	Percentage of Firms
Small-Scale Manufacturing:	
Plastics Manufacturing	12%
Electrical Components	8%
Construction	4%
Timber Processing	4%
Wood Working	8%
	Total: 36%
Service Activities:	
Real Estate	2%
Computer Technology	6%
Engineering Design	4%
Restaurant Operations	16%
Travel and Tourism	8%
Retailing	16%
Professional Services	12%
	Total: 64%

TABLE 3. Size of Small Business Venture

Number of Employees	Percentage of Firms
0-2	27.5%
3-5	21.6%
5-10	27.4%
10-30	7.8%
above 30	15.7%
	Total: 100.00%

management and/or distribution of the product. Table 3 shows that most of the growth of the private sector has been in the form of small and medium-size firms and individual entrepreneurship with employment starting from two employees to above thirty.

According to the survey results, Hungarian entrepreneurs had various reasons for starting their businesses. The most frequently mentioned motives were desire for wealth, need to control, and power, and followed by achievement, opportunity, challenge, and dissatisfaction with government jobs (Table 4). Respondents expressed that career security and a new political and economic climate played a strong role in their decisions to create entrepreneurial ventures.

The majority of entrepreneurs believed that they did not want any authority over them and they could do the job better than anyone; they need maximum responsibility and accountability to perform successfully. They envisaged a need for the freedom to initiate the action that they see as necessary for success. They also need to control and have power, as 74 percent of respondents stated, and to do their own things in their own ways. They enjoy creating and executing strategies. They see the future in their life as within their control and need to act in accordance with their own perception of what choices and action will result in achievement. Their achievement orientation and their abilities to solve problems overcome the majority of obstacles and difficulties encountered. They characterized themselves as having drive and achievement orientation and a constant uninterrupted pattern of behavior toward that achievement, and as being tireless in the pursuit of the goals they have set for themselves. They seem to be extremely clear in describing their immediate goals and how they will be achieved.

TABLE 4. Motivation for Involvement in Entrepreneurial Venture

Motivation	Percentage of Responses
Desire for Wealth	90.20%
Need for Control/Power	74.50%
Opportunity/Achievements	68.60%
Challenge	62.70%
Self-Interest/Gain	58.80%
Political/Economic Situation	52.90%
Creation of Something New	35.30%
Loss of Job/Job Frustration	29.40%
Family Interest/Background	27.50%
Career Security	23.50%

Table 5 and Table 6 present data on the perceived causes of business success and difficulties in running small businesses, and needed assistance for small business development in the country of study. All entrepreneurs surveyed indicated that they had encountered many problems with their businesses during start-up and the current operation.

Table 5 shows the perceived primary cause of business success. During the period of struggle for survival and growth, the entrepreneurs concentrated their resources and energies on essential expendi-

TABLE 5. Perceived Primary Cause of Business Success

External Factors	Percentage of Responses
Availability of Capital	74.50%
Availability of Supplies	58.80%
Business Contacts	82.40%
Customer Base	70.50%
Access to Information	62.70%
Technology/Equipment	54.90%
Internal Factors	
Professional Attitude	51.00%
Knowledge of Market	47.00%
Familiarity with Government Regulations	41.20%
Hard Work/Commitment	49.00%
Patience and Perseverance	47.00%

TABLE 6. Perceived Difficulties of Small Business Ventures

Perceived Difficulties	Percentage of Responses
Unstable Financial Market/High Interest Rates	90.20%
Inflation	82.40%
Unfavorable Credit Terms	78.40%
High Tax Burden	70.50%
Red Tape	55.00%
High Risk/	52.90%
Rapid Changes/Uncertainties	49.00%
Lack of Venture Capital	45.00%
Bad Infrastructure	74.50%
Lack of Access to Technology	58.80%
Cash Flow Problems	55.00%
Unfavorable Market Conditions	70.50%

tures for productive assets. They were aware that when starting and building a business, rapid growth was essential to achieve the size needed for stability and equilibrium. During the difficult periods of building their businesses, when resources were extremely scarce and limited and economic conditions very uncertain and unstable, they found their satisfaction in the performance of their businesses. According to interviewers, joint ventures are advantageous as they brought technology, managerial expertise and most importantly needed capital. They believe that greater promotion of foreign initiatives in Hungary through the founding of joint ventures and representation is very important at the early stage of their business growth since other sources of capital availability were extremely limited or impossible to obtain.

An important obstacle to the growth of small businesses in Hungary is the absence of a genuine banking system. The entrepreneurs complained that until 1987, banking was completely centralized, with commercial banking simply a branch of the central bank's activity. The central bank was merely an instrument of state planning and control over state-owned enterprises with its local branches. This assured that the enterprises maintained balance between investment, wages and working capital. As a consequence, the underdeveloped financial market has experienced significant problems in small venture creation and development.

Nevertheless, the major step along the way towards a more sound financial market was the establishment of the two-tier banking system on January 1987. The National Bank of Hungary was transformed into the Bank of Issue, and five commercial banks were established with licenses to conduct a wide range of banking operations, with the exception of banking transactions for the population and foreign exchange activities. This bank reform has ended the monopoly of the National Bank and established large commercial banks. Although the newly established, modern banking system provided a better financial environment, it still remained unsuitable for establishing market economy. Respondents complained that credit appraisal methods were absolute and could not create a sound basis for credit decisions. The level of computerization has been very low, and banks are unable to provide fast and efficient services. Most of the staff in the new banks come from the National Bank of Hungary and hence become used to a bureaucratic allocation of credits. The internal flow of information in the banks was generally very poor due to technical reasons and a monopolized information system. Entrepreneurs expressed that, in addition, the range of services and geographical dispersion and quality of services have been poor, and in order to increase private enterprise activity, a larger volume of credit must be made available by reducing the proportion of credits granted to the state budget. Other obstacles to small businesses included lack of business and financial training and difficulties in obtaining credit (Table 6). The most significant hindrance to private business activity is lack of capital and difficulties in obtaining credit. The financial sector in Hungary is fairly underdeveloped, interest rates are very high, and entrepreneurs are limited in their ability to obtain credit or preferential treatment. In order to obtain a loan, a small business owner must demonstrate a satisfactory plan and some credit history, and provide some collateral; most of the respondents did not establish credit history. In addition to limited access to credit, unfavorable credit terms with the high risk of borrowing and high level of inflation, and the inability of the banking system to make rapid international transactions further hampered small business growth and development (Table 6). Many respondents complained about the slow pace of changes in the financial sector. High nominal interest rates deterred most respondents from borrowing. Therefore, the majority of small businesses surveyed preferred retained earnings to outside capital for financing their investments. The impact of the real exchange rate appreciation that occurred early in 1992 and mid-1993 was a source of substantial dispute in Hungary with the majority of our respondents believing it to have been largely responsible for the poor trade performance of 1993/1994.

Credit insurance and exchange rate insurance have been extremely expensive due to the lack of specialized institutions. A further problem lies in the infrastructure; the data processing and the communicating systems in banks have not improved and on-line connection is still difficult.

Other current operating problems and concerns to Hungarian entrepreneurs were lack of access to technology, and unfavorable market conditions. The experiences gained from the struggles in the Communist era helped them guide their firms through the early stages successfully. Some admitted that they had little experience with organization, finance, marketing, planning or business operations. The majority indicated a great need for obtaining training in management, marketing, financing, accounting, and handling of cash flows (Table 7). A shortage of management skills may keep many small enterprises from achieving sustained growth, expansion and efficiency improvement. Attracting customers, lack of advertising, coping with increasing competition from domestic and foreign firms, and hiring competent workers created significant problems. The lack of business experience has caused the failure of some small businesses in the region.

The entrepreneurs would like assistance in financing and lower interest rates with fewer restrictions and collateral, and the government issuing preferential loans to small businesses and allowing for tax breaks and other preferences.

The study shows that the volatile economic environment hinders small business development and growth. Inflation rates are high, which further slows cash flow and investment activities. Stabilization policies are needed to maintain reasonable market conditions within which businesses feel secure to make decisions for the future.

Lack of skilled labor was seldom stated as a constraint at the time of establishment of the enterprise. Personal contacts and recommendations by friends and relatives were important modes of recruiting labor.

The study found a high degree of innovation and product change among the Hungarian small businesses surveyed. In terms of reasons for success, most of the respondents expressed that they have been adept in product innovation and the economic environment. About 95 percent of respondents who introduced new products or made improvements in existing businesses did so in response to increased foreign competition. In most cases the product change/improvement

TABLE 7. Perceived Assistance Need for Small Business Development

Desirable Assistance	Percent of Responses
Consulting and Management Expertise	74.50%
Venture Capital or Preferential Loans	72.50%
Technical Assistance/Western & Modern Technology	64.70%
Marketing Expertise/Advertising Practices	60.80%
Tax Advantages, Tax Breaks & Preferences	70.60%
Less Paper Work & Government Regulation	62.70%
Short Training Sessions in Management	56.80%
Examples of Marketing Studies	47.00%
Books, Trade Journals & Case Studies	35.30%

was considered successful and involved expansion of their businesses beyond the local markets. The development of distributions and marketing channels, availability of information about consumer preferences, market potentials and business contacts, and the presence of mcans for penetrating more distant markets were the main reasons behind growing competitive enterprises. Those small private owners who possessed managerial skills and experiences from previous management positions were able to anticipate business opportunities and consequences of decisions, do accurate accounting, and adjust to the new market-oriented mechanism.

It was also found that social factors were not hindering small business creation, organization, and development. Many of the respondents commented that they were never discouraged to start a business, as they reported somewhat favorable societal attitudes toward entrepreneurship. According to the majority, strong family and local community support played an important role in developing their small business ventures.

The majority of respondents held the opinion that the Hungarian government should have a significant role in assisting small business development and new venture creation. They expressed strongly that small business training and preferences to small businesses not only attract potential entrepreneurs to start a business but will develop societal awareness about the importance of entrepreneurs in the process of development and growth of emerging market economies (Table 7).

CONCLUSIONS

The Hungarian government realized that establishing an economy that relies on the logic, motivation, rules and coordination of the market would create realistic and united market conditions that would allow for economic growth and development and a full integration into the world market.

The emergence of a new private entrepreneurial initiative has led to the development of a private sector that became an essential part of the Hungarian economy. The growth of small-scale entrepreneurs in Hungary clearly eased some of the problems encountered in shifting to market economy. Understanding the entrepreneurs and their problems is thus vital to regional policy.

This paper finds that Hungarian entrepreneurs were triggered by environment when they immediately recognized opportunities that became available early in the reform process. Propensity to enterprise was found to be relatively high. Entrepreneurs had to develop very different skills from those they could rely on in the former system, and lots of new skills are yet to be acquired by entrepreneurs and the population alike. Hungarian entrepreneurs are educated, innovative, determined in the face of many problems, and strong proponents of a market economy.

The paper shows that Hungarian entrepreneurs have much difficulty in gaining access to the support networks necessary to launch successful new ventures. While basic liberties necessary for a market economy are legally provided, the institutional infrastructure of a market economy is deficient. The lack of an adequate banking system and an infrastructure supporting the creation, development and growth of small and medium-size enterprises creates a formidable barrier to entry and growth. Unprecise legislation and slow and incompetent bureaucracies hindered the growth of private economy. Difficulties in obtaining capital, unfavorable credit terms, and unstable market conditions with very high interest rates were cited as major obstacles in starting and operating businesses.

There certainly appears to be no special and comprehensive program to help the private sector. Nevertheless, entrepreneurs in Hungary proved to be successful due to their talents, skills, personal characteristics, and experiences gained from previous operations.

In order to be successful, Hungarian entrepreneurs have to continue to build and develop new products, markets, technologies, and methods of production and distribution, to invest in and improve quality, and provide value for their customers with the presence of strong government support programs, and developmental policies. Therefore, the government should contribute to entrepreneurship by adopting policies and regulations that provide a broader scope of opportunities to entrepreneurial growth and development. In particular, economic policies that allow people to more freely exercise their entrepreneurial talents are especially encouraged as these positively affect small business creation in the early stages of economic market development. Increased direct capital investment would further contribute to the acceleration of economic reorganization and the growth of the economy. To encourage foreign capital investment, government should offer large-scale tax allowance and open the entire sphere of production to private investment.

The government should also improve the socioeconomic dimension of the entrepreneurial environment. More technical, vocational training, short-term entrepreneurial development courses, and workshops/ seminars are needed to enhance business skills. Especially important is the offer of financial assistance to new venture creation and small business development. To combat problems that arise from poor infrastructure, small businesses may be given assistance by establishing incubator centers and industrial parks where resources and facilities can be shared.

A broad cultural acceptance of entrepreneurs and enterprising behavior is absent in Hungary. Understanding and accepting the risk-taking, uncertainty, and cultural-orientation inherent in entrepreneurial efforts will require major cultural changes for a society that was tightly controlled for over four decades. The government must create an "entrepreneurial culture" that enables firms to take risks.

In summary, this paper implies that the region's greatest promise lies in its human capital. For Hungary to continue to move toward an established market economy, it is important that the entrepreneurial sector be well established and that the newly created enterprises develop into strong international companies.

REFERENCES

Brockhouse, R.H. (1982). "The Psychology of the Entrepreneur." In C.A. Kent, D.L. Sexton, K.H. Vesper (Eds). *Encyclopedia of Entrepreneurship*. Englewood Cliffs, NJ: Prentice Hall, 39-57.

Gartner, W. B. (1989a). *Who is an Entrepreneur*. Entrepreneurship Theory and Practice. Summer: 47-67.

Gartner, W. B. (1989b). *Some Suggestions for Research on Entrepreneurial Traits and Characteristics. Entrepreneurship Theory and Practice*. Fall: 27-37.

Hornaday, J. and J. Abound. (1971). *Characteristics of Successful Entrepreneurs. Personnel Psychology.* 24: 141-153.

Hornaday, J. and C. Bunker. (1970). *The Nature of the Entrepreneur. Personnel Psychology.* 23: 45-54.

Jones, L. and J. Sakong. (1980). *Government, Business and Entrepreneurship in Economic Development: Korean Case.* Cambridge, MA: Harvard University Press.

Kent, C. A. (1984). *The Rediscovery of the Entrepreneur.* In "The Environment For Entrepreneurship." (Ed.) Calvin A. Kent. Lexington, Massachusetts, Toronto.

Kilby, P. (1971). *Entrepreneurship and Economic Development*. New York: The Free Press.

Schumpeter, J.A. (1934). *The Theory of Economic Development*. Cambridge, MA: Harvard University Press, 1934.

Sexton, D. L and R.W. Smilor. (1989). *The Art and Science of Entrepreneurship*. Cambridge: Ballinger Publishing Co.

Stevenson H. H. and D.E. Gumpert. (1985). *The Heart of Entrepreneurship. Harvard Business Review*. March-April: 85-94.

Tyson, L., T. Petri and H. Rogers. (1994). *Promoting Entrepreneurship in Eastern Europe. Small Business Economics*. 6, 165-184.

Zapalska, A. (1997a). *Profiles of Polish Entrepreneurship. Journal of Small Business Management*. 35, 2, April, 111-117.

Zapalska, A. (1997b). *A Profile of Woman Entrepreneur and Enterprises in Poland. Journal of Small Business Management*. 35, 4, October, 76-81.

Zapalska, A. and W. Mondal. (1997c). *The Role of the New Entrepreneurship in the New Emerging Market Economies: An Empirical Approach. A Case Study for Poland. Conference Proceedings of the 1997 American Association of Business and Behavioral Sciences*. February 1997.

SUBMITTED: 11/98
FIRST REVISION: 03/99
SECOND REVISION: 05/99
ACCEPTED: 07/99

Questionable Business Practices in Russia: Ethical Guidelines from Integrative Social Contracts Theory

Sheila M. Puffer

SUMMARY. This article applies Integrative Social Contracts Theory (Donaldson and Dunfee, 1994) to ethical issues in business situations in Russia arising between Russians and Westerners. The theory bases ethical decision making on universal hypernorms which are fundamental to human existence regardless of culture or nationality. Simultaneously, specific norms exist that may differ from one community or culture to another. The theory includes six criteria to help resolve conflicts among these different groups. This article uses a common situation of *blat* or personal favoritism in Russian business to illustrate how the theory can be applied to conflicting norms in interactions between Western business people and their counterparts in Central and Eastern European countries. *[Article copies available for a fee from The Haworth Document Delivery Service: 1-800-342-9678. E-mail address: getinfo@haworthpressinc.com <Website: http://www.haworthpressinc.com>]*

KEYWORDS. Russia, ethical issues in business, changing values, East-West culture clash, changing institutions

A well-developed infrastructure supporting ethical business practices is an essential underpinning of every viable economic system. Yet,

Sheila M. Puffer is Professor at Northeastern University, College of Business Administration, 325 Hayden Hall, Boston, MA 02115 USA (e-mail: spuffer@cba.neu.edu).

[Haworth co-indexing entry note]: "Questionable Business Practices in Russia: Ethical Guidelines from Integrative Social Contracts Theory." Puffer, Sheila M. Co-published simultaneously in *Journal of East-West Business* (International Business Press, an imprint of The Haworth Press, Inc.) Vol. 5, No. 4, 1999, pp. 23-36; and: *Strategic Management in Central and Eastern Europe* (ed: Peter Geib, and Lucie Pfaff) International Business Press, an imprint of The Haworth Press, Inc., 2000, pp. 23-36. Single or multiple copies of this article are available for a fee from The Haworth Document Delivery Service [1-800-342-9678, 9:00 a.m. - 5:00 p.m. (EST). E-mail address: getinfo@haworthpressinc.com].

blatant examples of unethical or questionable business practices exist in all societies, and business practitioners must resolve ethical dilemmas as an integral aspect of their jobs.

Many Western academics and business people are in strong agreement with their counterparts in Central and Eastern Europe that creating a sound business infrastructure is a top priority in order for the region to develop its economic potential both domestically and internationally. While conducting business in an ethical manner is the unquestioned objective, what constitutes ethical behavior is not always readily apparent. It is especially difficult to agree on what is ethical when individuals from different cultures try to find common ground. Western views of ethical behavior do not necessarily fit the different historical, political, economic, and social conditions in Central and Eastern Europe, and differences also exist among various Central and Eastern European countries themselves.

It is widely recognized that ethical issues, particularly those that arise in cross-cultural and international business transactions, are often colored by a host of contingencies relating to the nature of the situation, the stakes or consequences involved, the national culture of the individuals engaged in the activity, and other environmental factors (DeGeorge, 1993; Donaldson, 1989). Seldom can an easy solution be found to complex problems.

OBJECTIVES OF THIS ARTICLE

The focus of this article is on an ethical framework called Integrative Social Contracts Theory, which was recently developed by Professors Thomas Donaldson and Thomas Dunfee of the Wharton School of Business at the University of Pennsylvania. After presenting an overview of the framework, I will illustrate how it can be used to analyze and resolve ethical issues in business situations in Russia arising between Russians and Westerners. The theory bases ethical decision making on universal hypernorms which are fundamental to human existence regardless of culture or nationality. These hypernorms, such as core human rights, respect for human dignity, and good citizenship, are the minimum threshold for ethical behavior. Simultaneously, specific norms exist that may differ from one community or culture to another. The theory includes six criteria to help resolve conflicts among these different groups. My analysis will include examples from the Russian context as an illustration of how the theory can be applied to conflicting norms in interactions between Western business people and their counterparts in Central and Eastern European countries.

First, an overview of the political and economic environment of Russian business will be provided. I will then briefly review a framework for categorizing the commonalities and differences in ethical perspectives on business activities, as illustrated by attitudes of Russians and Americans. Next, I will apply the integrative contracts theory to a vignette prepared by an American observer, based on a real-life situation he recently documented in Russian business. Comments about the case by two Russian colleagues who have extensive experience in the Russian business environment will also be presented.

POLITICAL AND ECONOMIC ENVIRONMENT OF RUSSIAN BUSINESS

Business ethics is a focal issue in all the transitional economies of Central and Eastern Europe and the former Soviet republics. Each country has its unique features, and ethical practices emerge from the types of business infrastructure that have been developed, including standardized business practices and contracts, a code of business law, legal institutions, trade associations and industrial groups, and government lobbies. The countries undergoing these dramatic economic transformations from central planning to a more market-oriented system have evolved at different rates, and each has its own primary concerns. Poland, the Czech Republic, and Hungary are generally recognized as having made the most progress, and are positioning themselves as members of NATO and the European Union. And the major focus in the reunified German Republic is on the differentials found in the eastern and western sectors in such crucial areas as unemployment, productivity, and collectivist versus individualist values in the workplace.

As for Russia, this country of 170 million people is widely regarded as having made the slowest progress of any major country toward market reforms. Throughout the decade of the 1990s, the country has experienced many setbacks and failures, including a failed policy of privatization of former state-owned enterprises, oppressive and confusing tax legislation, erratic law enforcement, and policies generally unfavorable to foreign investment. Finally, the government's default on international and domestic debts in August 1998 paralyzed the economy, causing a rash of bank failures and choking off funds to conduct business transactions. Essentially, the August crisis marked the end of an era, as the Russian business newspaper, *Kommersant*, announced in a headline. The era of market reforms came to an abrupt end. The government, headed by the newly appointed prime minister Evgeny Primakov, tightened its grip on the country by giving a stronger role to the Central Bank and developing policies to renationalize many enterprises in key industrial and natural resource sectors.

The chaotic and anarchic political and economic environment in which business has been conducted in Russia for the past decade has created great uncertainty about what constitutes ethical business practices. Additionally, few institutions have been developed to set policies and procedures and to enforce laws pertaining to business transactions. In this vacuum, coupled with unique historical, political, and cultural characteristics, the criminal element has virtually taken over the economy, to such an extent that some analysts have said that Russia is one of the most corrupt countries in the world (Filipov, 1998).

This corruption has come from two sources: the criminal mafia and the new nomenklatura class. The criminal mafia is pervasive in the economic as well as political arenas. For instance, the Tambov clan is reputed to control import and export operations in St. Petersburg, and to have penetrated law enforcement agencies, thereby giving them immunity from prosecution (Filipov, 1998). The second source of corruption is the nomenklatura group of bankers, industrialists, and government officials who colluded to gain power and build financial and industrial conglomerates. Prior to the country's 1998 economic collapse, they amassed fortunes by acquiring state assets for extremely low prices, stifling competition, and receiving annual interest rates of windfall proportions on government securities, typically in excess of 100 percent. Many of the heads of these conglomerates, who came to be known as oligarchs, saw their empires virtually destroyed in the wake of the country's 1998 financial crisis. For instance, the $3.7 billion in assets held by Vladimir Potanin's Onexim Bank group in early 1998 were virtually wiped out a year later, and the conglomerate was nearly $2 billion in debt (Kranz, 1999).

The Russian business environment in the first quarter of 1999 was characterized by great uncertainty and hardship, with the major emphasis being on trying to recover from the August 1998 crisis. While former oligarchs such as Potanin were attempting to restructure their conglomerates, the government was struggling to keep the country and its citizens from the brink of economic and social chaos. The country was in financial ruin, with woefully inadequate tax collection and law enforcement efforts, and capital flight has been estimated at $140 billion from 1992 to 1997 (Reddaway, 1998). A harsh winter, coupled with the worst harvest in years, exacerbated the suffering of average citizens, and President Yeltsin's tenuous political and physical health were the focus of much speculation.

All of these circumstances combine to create a highly uncertain environment for people trying to do business in Russia. As former Soviet president Mikhail Gorbachev summarized in a recent interview: "The situation in Russia must be stabilized. It is continuing to unravel, and we have not yet stopped the unraveling . . . and 90 percent of the population is calling for [Yeltsin's] resignation. . . . In this situation, I think we'll see a new political center emerging. Not a leftist center, but a [moderate] center" (Puffer, 1999: 12-13).

So far, I have referred primarily to the activities of the government and the elite class of oligarchs who built huge banking and industrial empires throughout the 1990s. However, the business people who are the focus of my discussion of business ethics consist of the broad group of individuals who operate state-owned enterprises, semi-privatized or privatized enterprises, and newly formed entrepreneurships. In contrast to the oligarchs, these individuals have had to find ways of doing business largely without the benefit of highly placed government contacts or access to generous credit lines. In this confusing environment, no single set of business ethics has yet emerged. Some observers describe at least two distinct sets of ethics, one which blatantly disregards ethical constraints, and another which observes generally accepted universal ethical norms (Anderson and Shikhirev, 1994).

CASE STUDY: THE TOURIST TRAP

One company that is trying to operate a modest business at a reasonable profit is Russtravel (adapted from Thelen, 1999). It is about to enter a joint venture with a small American airline called Sloan Air.

Russtravel does business in ways that many Russian businesses do. Financial transactions are priced in dollars and paid in cash or by wire transfer. The company is four years old, highly automated, and staffed with multi-lingual representatives who are sensitive to customers' needs. The high level of customer service is evident from the large number of repeat customers the firm has in a competitive market.

Sloan Air, a small American airline, caters to private, upscale vacationers. The company has had much success in North America and Europe. Believing that the Moscow and St. Petersburg markets are saturated with Russian and Western airlines and travel agencies, they decided to explore other cities to increase their customer base. The growing number of wealthy "New Russians" in medium-sized cities had opened up a market for upscale tourists interested in vacationing in desirable Mediterranean locations such as Spain, the United Arab Emirates, Turkey, and Tunisia. Sloan Air hoped to find Russian travel agencies that would offer travelers its vacation packages.

One potential partner they located was called Russtravel. Sloan began exploring opportunities with the Russian travel agency which was located in an attractive medium-sized city that had a reasonable number of affluent citizens. After several months of contacts and negotiations, Sloan Air and Russtravel decided to enter into a 50-50 joint venture.

At the celebration party, prior to signing the contract, Russtravel's managing director took his prospective American partner into his office and told her about the company's financial situation. He admitted that the firm did not record approximately 30 percent of its sales, amounting to half its cash transactions, in order to avoid paying taxes. He added that the tax inspector had been auditing the firm for the past week. Overall, the inspector concluded that the books were fine. The tax inspector did not make any mention of the hidden transactions, but did uncover some minor procedural errors.

The tax inspector stated openly that these procedural errors would be ignored if Russtravel paid a bribe to him personally, as well as a small fine that would make his audit look good to his bosses. The total of the fine and the bribe was approximately half the amount of the legitimate fines that the inspector could levy if he were inclined to do so. The inspector also stated that he had not audited the books as closely as he could have, and that he could arrange to be in charge of Russtravel's tax audit the following year. Thus, a bribe would again be necessary at that time. The advantage to Russtravel was that they would know with whom they were dealing in future.

Russtravel's managing director assumed that this situation was common in many countries and asked Sloan Air's general manager how American firms typically handled such incidents. She explained that this was not a common practice for American companies, although it did occur on occasion. She added that the U.S. government's Foreign Corrupt Practices Act prohibited American companies from paying bribes. She was also confident that Sloan Air had not paid bribes in any of the markets where it operated. The Sloan Air general manager was aware that Russtravel's experience with the tax inspectors was a common occurrence in Russia, and that the joint venture she was considering with Russtravel could be subject to the same inspection and bribe solicitation as Russtravel had experienced. What action should be taken by the prospective American partner?

A CROSS-CULTURAL FRAMEWORK FOR BUSINESS PRACTICES

To help answer this question, a first step would be to utilize a framework published several years ago to classify cross-cultural business activities (Puffer and McCarthy, 1995). Business practices can be categorized according to how ethical they are viewed in each country. Differences in ethical perspectives arise from a wide range of historical, cultural, political, legislative, economic, and social forces that shape individuals' mindsets (Puffer, McCarthy, and Zhuplev, 1996). Practices that are seen as ethical in both countries, or unethical in both countries, are typically quite easy to resolve, since the two parties agree on the nature of the practices. This occurs, for instance, in the case of keeping one's word, which is considered an ethical practice in both Russia and the United States. The same applies for such blatantly unethical and illegal practices as gangsterism, racketeering, and extortion.

In contrast, the most challenging and sometimes contentious issues represent incongruent views about the ethicality of various business practices. For instance, manipulating or misrepresenting data is typically viewed as unethical by Americans, but often considered ethical, or at least a fairly commonly accepted business practice, in Russia. Likewise, layoffs may be viewed as ethical, or at least a common business practice in the United States, but are more likely to be viewed as unethical in Russia.

APPLYING THE INTEGRATIVE SOCIAL CONTRACTS THEORY

Returning to the case of Russtravel and Sloan Air, two business issues can be viewed as having ethical implications. First, the fact that Russtravel does not pay its full tax bill may be considered an example of manipulating data, or of ignoring senseless laws and regulations. Second, Russtravel is considering offering bribes or grease payments to reduce its tax bill. As seen in Table 2, all of these practices are viewed differently by Russians and Americans, with Russians generally considering them ethical or at least common business practice, and Americans considering them as being unethical. The question then arises: which set of ethics should apply? Given that business is being conducted on Russian soil, decisions might follow the adage, When in Rome, do as the Romans do. Yet, Americans are prohibited by their own government from engaging in bribery in any part of the world.

The integrative social contracts theory developed by Thomas Donaldson and Thomas Dunfee (1994) is a useful technique for analyzing such divergent ethical perspectives and suggesting an ethically-defensible solution. An important feature of the theory is that different behaviors are recognized as existing in different groups or communities. The six principles for evaluating the ethicality of behavior are listed in Table 1. In an application of the theory, I will focus on the controversial ethical issue of grease payments or *blat,* as it is termed in Russian, and will draw from a recent chapter on the subject (Puffer and McCarthy, 1998: 432-433). The application of the six rules to the issue of *blat* is outlined in Table 2.

Personal favoritism, known as *blat,* involves "reliance for favors upon personal contacts with people in influential positions" (Puffer and McCarthy, 1995: 37). *Blat* takes many forms, such as giving money, goods, or services to people in power who can help the givers receive or achieve something they value such as a job, promotion, contract, or access to influential people. Securing favors can sometimes involve payments to a series of individuals who are instrumental in gaining access to the final decision maker. *Blat* has for centuries been a common practice in Russia, but it is considered bribery and illegal

TABLE 1. Six Principles for Evaluating the Ethicality of Behavior (from Donaldson and Dunfee, 1994)

Rule 1. Transactions solely within a single community, which do not have significant adverse effects on other humans or communities, should be governed by the host community's norms.

Rule 2. Community norms indicating a preference for how conflict-of-norms situations should be resolved should be applied, so long as they do not have significant adverse effects on other humans or communities.

Rule 3. The more extensive or more global the community which is the source of the norm, the greater the priority which should be given to the norm.

Rule 4. Norms essential to the maintenance of the economic environment in which the transaction occurs should have priority over norms potentially damaging to that environment.

Rule 5. Where multiple conflicting norms are involved, patterns of consistency among the alternative norms provide a basis for prioritization.

Rule 6. Well-defined norms should ordinarily have priority over more general, less precise norms.

TABLE 2. Evaluating the Ethicality of Grease Payments or *Blat*

Rule 1: Ethical
Blat is pervasive in Russian society, so can be considered a norm in business.

Rule 2: Ethical
Blat does not conflict with other norms, unless it increases to the point of illegal bribery.

Rule 3: Ethical
Blat is consistent with the social norm of gift giving.

Rule 4: Ethical
Blat is not damaging to the economic system, and may facilitate business, but if it turns into bribery, it would harm the economic system.

Rule 5: Ethical
Many Russians view *blat* as violating the principle of basic fairness, but oppressive conditions have often made *blat* necessary for survival.

Rule 6: Ethical
Blat has long been a well-defined norm ad accepted as almost inevitable, given political repression and limited freedom of opportunity.

CONCLUSION: *Blat* would generally be considered ethical by the Russian business community, although many would consider it as being unfair, as easily turning into bribery, and conflicting with Western business practices.

when large amounts of money are involved or highly placed authorities blatantly abuse their power. A number of tax collectors, for instance, have been prosecuted during the transition for taking large bribes from taxpayers in exchange for favorable treatment (Rudskii, 1996).

Historical conditions which encouraged *blat* included the expectation that serfs would bring gifts to the landowner to gain favor and avoid sanctions. And in the broader Russian society, gift giving has been a widely accepted and expected practice. For instance, gifts are frequently exchanged in business and personal relationships, such as when visiting companies and homes. Gifts help to bind friendships, gain cooperation, and secure specific favors. Severe shortages of goods and limited opportunities for individual rewards during the Communist period further contributed to the use of *blat*. For instance, individuals would exchange favors such as accepting goods from an enterprise manager in return for facilitating his child's admission to a university. In the more market-oriented economy, *blat* could be used to improve one's business, by seeking favors like gaining access to bank financing, securing preferential terms in contracts, or winning access to important customers.

Because *blat* has been so pervasive within Russian society as a whole, it could also be considered a norm of the business communities, and thus ethical (Rule 1). Similarly, community norms do not bring *blat* into conflict with other norms, and thus it is considered legitimate until it reaches the point of being illegal bribery (Rule 2). Similar to Rule 1, the broader community's endorsement of gift giving is consistent with the practice of *blat* in business (Rule 3). *Blat* in itself is not damaging to the economic system of Russia, and may even facilitate business transactions in a traditionally bureaucratic society. Thus it can be considered legitimate unless it would harm the economic system such as when bribery occurs (Rule 4). The practice of *blat* is consistent with other norms that are considered ethical. These include building networks of relatives and friends who are reliable and trustworthy, and refraining from whistleblowing to protect oneself and others against the arbitrary use of power and punishment by authorities.

However, *blat* would be considered by many Russians to be inconsistent with the norm of basic fairness, but the oppressive conditions under which they lived have promoted *blat* as a necessity for survival

(Rule 5). *Blat* has long been a well-defined norm and accepted as almost inevitable given the lack of freedom and opportunity under oppressive political regimes (Rule 6).

> Applying all six rules of social integrative contracts theory, *blat* emerges as an accepted, and generally, legitimate practice within Russia that developed as a mechanism for survival under harsh conditions. However, many Russians would not consider it to be fair, and under other circumstances would likely see it as unethical. As Russia becomes more of a market economy, tied more tightly to the global economy, the ethicality of *blat* is likely to come into question. For instance, in doing business with Americans, the Foreign Corrupt Practices Act which regulates Americans' behavior would likely limit the use of *blat* by Russians in transactions with Americans. (Puffer and McCarthy, 1998: 432-433)

WHAT SHOULD BE DONE IN THE TOURIST TRAP CASE?

Based on this analysis of grease payments or *blat*, a case can be made that the prospective American partner Sloan Air, in the Tourist Trap case, should simply accept the situation as explained by Russtravel and go along with payments to the tax inspector. However, a fine line exists between *blat* and bribery, and many Russian firms also want to be seen as legitimate and respectable business partners with Western counterparts. To examine this controversial issue more thoroughly, I called upon two Russian colleagues to give their views of this commonly encountered business situation. One colleague is Chief Operating Officer of Beeline-Wimpel Communications in Moscow, and the other is currently a business school faculty member at an American university. Both colleagues are highly knowledgeable and experienced in the Russian as well as the American business environment.

These experts noted several alternatives for the Sloan Air general manager to consider. First, she could simply go along with Russtravel's assessment of the situation and tell the director to pay the tax inspector as he proposed. However, this decision would likely lead to similar actions in the new joint venture and make both the Russian and American partners vulnerable to fines or other government repercussions. It could also have a political backlash for the American firm that might be accused of bribing so-called honest tax inspectors. At the other extreme, the American firm could take illegal and unethical measures to try to make as much money as possible and avoid paying high taxes, then close the business and leave the Russian partner to face the consequences alone.

If the American general manager were to insist on strictly complying with the U.S. Foreign Corrupt Practices Act and refusing to accept questionable tax practices, ethical issues would be eliminated. However, Russtravel's director might become alienated if he felt pressured to accept the American's decision without sufficient regard for his own circumstances. Such a reaction could undermine the trust in the partners' business relationship.

Two solutions were seen by the experts as being the best choices, and both involved compliance with Russian and American laws. The American general manager should explain why making payments to the tax inspector is unethical as well as bad for business, but leave the decision to the Russian partner as a sign of respect, and to give him a sense of ownership of the consequences. The joint venture should avoid paying bribes in both the short and long term, and Sloan Air's management in the United States should be informed of the business conditions in Russia. Additionally, operating procedures should be developed by the joint venture to have the Russian partner responsible for effectively handling sensitive aspects of domestic operations, including interactions with the tax inspection service. In summary, the experts viewed this scenario as being fairly common, and concluded that an ethical approach could likely be worked out between the partners if they were able to build a relationship of trust and mutual respect.

CONCLUSION

In conclusion, this article has described some of the characteristics of the current economic and political situation in Russia that create a challenging context in which to conduct business in an ethical manner. Two frameworks have been discussed as techniques for analyzing ethical issues. These are the classification framework developed by Puffer and McCarthy, as well as the integrative social contracts theory developed by Donaldson and Dunfee. A commonly encountered business incident was used to illustrate how these frameworks can be applied in real-life situations, and various solutions proposed by two Russian colleagues to resolve the case were discussed. In summary, despite the difficult conditions currently in effect in Russia, it is hoped that the frameworks discussed here can be useful points of departure for creating ethical business practices between Russian and Western partners.

Finally, the approach taken by a Norwegian millionaire who profitably operated boats between Moscow and St. Petersburg offers a valuable lesson in business ethics in a highly unstable transitional economic environment. When asked about the key to his success, he replied: "I had one success factor–never do unethical things. I had to walk away from many doors empty-handed, to refuse many promising proposals, but I never bribed a person in Russia. It pays to be honest in the end."

REFERENCES

Anderson, R., & Shikhirev, P. (1994). *"Akuly" i "del'finy": Psikhologiia i etika rossiisko-amerikanskogo delovogo partnerstva ("Sharks" and "Dolphins": The psychology and ethics of Russian and American business partnerships)*. Moscow: Delo.

DeGeorge, R. (1986). *Competing with integrity in international business*. New York: Oxford University Press.

Donaldson, T. (1989). *The ethics of international business*. New York: Oxford University Press.

Donaldson, T., & Dunfee, T. (1994). Toward a unified conception of business ethics: Integrative social contracts theory. *Academy of Management Review, 19* (2), 252-284.

Filipov, D. (1998). Rule by decree fought in St. Petersburg. *Boston Sunday Globe*, December 6, p. A8.

Kranz, P. Fall of an oligarch. *Business Week*, March 1, 1999, pp. 44-45.

Puffer, S.M. (1999). Mikhail Gorbachev on globalization. *The Academy of Management Executive, 13* (1): 8-14.

Puffer, S.M., & McCarthy, D.J. (1995). Finding the common ground in Russian and American business ethics. *California Management Review, 37* (2), 29-46.

Puffer, S.M., & McCarthy, D.J. (1998). Business ethics in a transforming economy: Applying the integrative social contracts theory to Russia. In B.N. Kumar and H. Steinmann (eds.), *Ethics in International Management*. Berlin: de Gruyter, 419-438.

Puffer, S.M., McCarthy, D.J., & Zhuplev, A.V. (1996). Meeting of the mindsets in a changing Russia, *Business Horizons, 39* (6), 52-60.

Reddaway, P. (1998). The roots of Russia's crisis: The Soviet legacy, IMF/G7 policies, and Yeltsin's authoritarianism: Where is the crisis now leading? *Russian Business Watch, 3* (6), 12-15.

Rudskii, L. (1996). Podarok . . . vziatka (Gift . . . bribe). *Novoe Russkoe Slovo*, July 20-21, p. 17.

Thelen, S. (1999). Five Russian business cases. Unpublished manuscript. Norfolk, Virginia: Old Dominion University.

SUBMITTED: 03/99
FIRST REVISION: 04/99
SECOND REVISION: 05/99
ACCEPTED: 07/99

Internationalisation of Hypermarket Retailing in Poland: West European Investment and Its Implications

John Dawson
John Henley

SUMMARY. Retailing in Poland after 1989 was privatised rapidly. There was an explosion in the number of small shops and kiosks. By 1996 rationalisation had begun in the store network. By the mid-1990s foreign retailers were perceiving the Polish market as a potentially lucrative one. Several store formats were introduced. Hypermarket operators from Western Europe have moved into the market strongly since the mid-1990s. French and German retailers are making substantial investments in this format. There are notable implications for the supply chain, logistics and the behaviour of manufacturers of fast-moving consumer goods, particularly food. There are implications also for the training and development of a cadre of managers in operational and strategic functions. The development of hypermarkets represents a significant transfer of managerial know-how from Western to Central Eu-

John Dawson is Professor of Marketing, The Management School/University of Edinburgh, 50 George Square, Edinburgh EH8 9JY, Scotland (e-mail: John.Dawson@ed.ac.uk).

John Henley is Professor of International Management at the University of Edinburgh, Scotland.

The authors gratefully acknowledge the support of the ACE Phare Programme of EU who funded the research on which this paper is based. The research is based on interviews with retailer and support services during 1996 through 1998.

[Haworth co-indexing entry note]: "Internationalisation of Hypermarket Retailing in Poland: West European Investment and Its Implications." Dawson, John, and John Henley. Co-published simultaneously in *Journal of East-West Business* (International Business Press, an imprint of The Haworth Press, Inc.) Vol. 5, No. 4, 1999, pp. 37-52; and: *Strategic Management in Central and Eastern Europe* (ed: Peter Geib and Lucie Pfaff) International Business Press, an imprint of The Haworth Press, Inc., 2000, pp. 37-52. Single or multiple copies of this article are available for a fee from The Haworth Document Delivery Service [1-800-342-9678, 9:00 a.m. - 5:00 p.m. (EST). E-mail address: getinfo@haworthpressinc.com].

37

rope. There are also implications for the small shopkeeper sector which has already been affected but is likely to be more heavily affected as hypermarket numbers increase. In the process of the modernisation of retailing in Poland foreign hypermarket operators are playing an important role. *[Article copies available for a fee from The Haworth Document Delivery Service: 1-800-342-9678. E-mail address: getinfo@haworthpressinc.com <Website: http://www.haworthpressinc.com>]*

KEYWORDS. Retail, hypermarkets, internationalisation, Poland, retail evolution

INTRODUCTION

West European retailers have made substantial moves into Poland since 1993. These moves have created some particular issues in strategic management for the in-coming firms, for the indigenous retailers and for both Polish and multinational suppliers of goods and services. The aim of this paper is to consider the effects of this move into Poland by retailers from Western Europe, with particular reference to large hypermarkets selling food and non-food goods. The research is based on a programme of interviews conducted with retailers and suppliers through 1996 to 1998.

The reasons for the strong attraction of the Polish retail sector for West European retail investors are clear. Poland has experienced the fastest expansion of GDP in continental Europe since 1994 with GDP growth rates in excess of 5% per annum (pa) rising to 7% pa in 1997. Perhaps more importantly, private consumption has been rising even faster than GDP, reaching 8.2% pa in 1996. There is, however, some concern about the trade gap which partly reflects this explosion of private consumption sucking in imports. The trade gap is currently growing at an unsustainable rate, up from $11 bn in 1996 to $14 bn in 1997. Fortunately the deficit on the current account is covered by capital account inflows. Thus the stock of foreign direct investment in Poland had risen to $20.6 bn in 1997 up from $13.7 bn in 1996, and $8.5 bn in 1995. Poland now leads other Central and East European [CEE] countries as the preferred destination for foreign direct investment, a comforting endorsement for existing and prospective international retail investors.

From a retail perspective, within CEE countries, Poland is attractive for several reasons. It has a large population, exceeded only by Russia and the Ukraine in CEE, of 38.6 million. This population is relatively young: 38 per cent are under 25 years of age and only 11 per cent are over 65 years old. While Poland was afflicted with near hyper-inflation in 1990 after the collapse of communism, today price inflation is being brought down to EU standards. By the end of 1997 the annualised rate was down to 13.2% and the forecast for 1998 is 11.0%. While average real disposable income is growing fast, up from a rate of 5.7% pa in 1996 to 6.5% pa in 1997, the average Polish household still spends over 30% of the family budget on food. Alongside the general growth there remain considerable regional disparities in infrastructure and in consumer spending (Chojnicki, Cryz and Parysek 1999). Poland is thus attractive to both food retailers and non-food retailers seeking to capture this growing consumer spending power.

Moreover, political risk is declining with Poland's accession to membership of OECD in 1996 and NATO in 1997 and the beginning of formal negotiations for full EU membership on 1 April 1998. Of course, Poland's economic development is still vulnerable to fall out from the Russian economic and political crisis even though the EU dominates trade relations: two-thirds of Polish exports go to the EU. However, a significant 7% of exports still go to Russia and 4% to Ukraine which Poland can ill-afford to lose given its worsening trade gap.

In the first section of this paper we provide a brief overview of the development of retailing in Poland. The remainder of this paper provides an assessment of international investment in hypermarkets, considers the implications of this investment for the Polish retail economy and seeks to examine the extent of the internationalisation of this one segment of the retail sector.[1]

PRESENT POSITION OF RETAILING

Fundamental changes in retailing followed the change in political systems in 1989 (Martin, 1997, Corporate Intelligence 1996). Johnson and Loveman (1995) point to the importance of retailing in early attempts to create a private sector and also describe the complex process of privatisation. Legal regulations introduced since 1989 have resulted in:

- the abolition of many controls over the distribution and pricing of goods;
- introduction of free market principles across almost all the retail sector;
- privatisation of state-run trading enterprises;
- low entry barriers for new businesses and a consequent rapid growth of small firms;
- liberalisation of many of the regulations governing commercial practices.

The consequence is that less than one per cent of stores are now in state ownership and about 6 per cent are owned by consumer co-operatives with the remainder being in the private sector.

The Store Network

The growth in number of stores and in the total number of retail outlets has been considerable. This is shown in Table 1. From this table it can be seen that the main growth took place after 1989 with a very rapid growth in numbers of stalls, kiosks and mobile retail outlets in the early 1990s. By 1996 there were over 520,000 of this form of outlet. Official figures for 1997 are not available but non-official views are that this informal retailing is declining with some moving into the formal sector. The number of fixed stores has also increased but now is oscillating around 420,000.

TABLE 1. The Retail Network in Poland

Year	Total number of sales points '000	Number of stores '000
1980	203.7	129.9
1985	219.8	142.1
1990	469.7	237.4
1991	630.0	311.0
1992	700.0	352.5
1993	785.0	380.6
1994	850.0	415.4
1995	890.0	425.6
1996	927.0	405.6
1997		424.4

Source: Central Statistical Office Annual Report on Retail Trade

The size of these fixed shops is small. Table 2 shows the size distribution of stores. It is noticeable that the number of small stores no longer increases consistently year on year. There are now signs that the shop network is starting to rationalise with a reduction in the total number of retail outlets seen in 1996 and although the 1997 figures show an increase this is in part the result of the formalisation of informal kiosk-style retailing. The pattern of evolution follows a model of rapid growth to satisfy pent-up consumer demand and now competitive processes are starting to work to reduce the number of small stores and informal retailing with increased numbers of large stores often operated by foreign retailers (Company Assistance, 1997, 1998).

This process of competitive concentration is at a very early stage. Table 3 shows the number of firms related to the number of fixed stores they operate. The number of very small firms showed a decrease in 1996 but again a small increase in 1997. More importantly the number of firms developing small chains of up to 10 stores has

TABLE 2. The Size Distribution of Stores

Year	Number of stores '000	< 50 sq.m.	51-100 sq.m.	101-200 sq.m.	201-300 sq.m.	301-400 sq.m.	> 400 sq.m.
1993	380.6	347,650	19,875	8189	2075	867	1926
1994	415.4	383,064	10,421	8072	2035	863	1994
1995	425.6	391,297	20,268	8563	2238	1003	2231
1996	405.6	369,926	20,661	8929	2377	1110	2560
1997	424.4	387,921	20,583	9175	2570	1255	2858

Source: Central Statistical Office Annual Report on Retail Trade

TABLE 3. Number of Firms by Size of Store Network

Year	1-2 stores	3-10 stores	11-20 stores	21-50 stores	51-100 stores	101-200 stores	over 200 stores
1991	254,867	2211	1239	882	91	11	5
1992	306,318	2604	1244	559	54	10	3
1993	328,352	2787	1142	479	39	7	3
1994	365,998	3114	1054	409	31	7	3
1995	377,547	3989	969	337	27	4	2
1996	358,482	4504	882	290	23	5	2
1997	375,762	4689	866	248	23	3	3

Source: Central Statistical Office Annual Report on Retail Trade

increased steadily. The decrease in numbers of larger firms relates to the break up of privatized state chains which have been unable to respond to the new trading conditions. The new entrepreneurs in retailing are often still of a size to grow their business by the addition of single stores and are in the size category of 3-10 stores. A small number of the larger firms are very successful and are absorbing competitors so reducing the number of larger firms.

Estimated retail sales in 1996 were 57.6 billion ECU. Food and alcohol retailing accounted for 48% of retail sales in 1990 but by 1997 this had fallen to 41%. This is still high by West European standards but the decrease of food in total retail sales continues steadily (EUROSTAT 1998a). The gradual increase in spending power of consumers is encouraging the emergence of new non-food stores. In this, however, it must be appreciated that per capita retail spending is presently less than 1500 ECU which is below that in the Czech Republic and less than a third that of the per capita figure in Germany or France (Bauer and Carman 1996; Seitz 1992; EUROSTAT 1998b). It is potential growth which is driving the entrepreneurial ambitions of Polish retailers and also is seen as very attractive by German, French and British retailers who are entering Poland.

Foreign Retailers

Although not large in number the influence of foreign retailers is substantial (Pütz 1997). The challenges presented by foreign retailers are associated with their access to larger capital reserves than domestic retailers, their experience and expertise in operating highly efficient retail formats, their view of the distribution channel being retailer rather than supplier led, and their the greater awareness of consumer demands. These all enhance the ability of foreign retailers to compete successfully against domestically based retailers in the context of Poland.

In 1996 the Institute of Home Market and Consumption (1997) estimated there were 925 stores operated by foreign retailers and emphasized that their number belied their importance. The number more than doubled between 1996 and 1998. Several of the major hypermarket and supermarket companies, for example, Carrefour, Metro, Casino and Tesco, have begun development of stores in Poland and have ambitious opening programmes. In the non-food sector the entrants from outside Poland have been less dramatic but in some cases very significant, for example, IKEA. Foreign retailers have been important as catalysts for retail restructuring (Domanski 1996; Pütz 1998a,b).

Considering the activity of foreign retailers so far in their development, it is possible to posit a simple three-phase model of development.

Phase 1: Pioneering. These are companies which entered Polish retailing in the early 1990s when the market was very unstable, inflation was high and trading conditions chaotic. At this time they gained valuable experience of the Polish cultural and commercial environments and have been able to build on the early experience. Illustrative of the Pioneers are IKEA, Billa, REMA 1000, Yves Rocher, Rossman and Makro. IKEA have been sourcing products from Polish furniture manufacturers for 30 years and in the early 1990s opened three stores in quick succession. The number of stores has grown more steadily with seven in operation by mid-1998. Importantly IKEA is developing its stores as part of shopping centre complexes into which other foreign retailers are attracted. GIB entered in 1991 buying four supermarkets in Warsaw. Billa entered in 1990 and developed supermarkets particularly in Warsaw and Bielsko-Biala initially. REMA entered in 1993 through a form of franchise system to target the discount food market. Rossman was an early entrant into the discount drugstore sector. Makro opened its first store in 1994 in Warsaw and has expanded considerably since then. Several pioneers have been successful in expanding their store network, for example, REMA 1000 with 44 stores in 1997, Rossman with 22 stores in 1997, so becoming established. In a few cases, for example, GIB with only 11 stores by 1997, there has been difficulty establishing a reasonable market presence and in other cases external activity, for example, Billa's [10 stores in 1997] purchase by Rewe, has slowed development.

Phase 2: Colonisation. By 1995 the potential of Poland was starting to be realised and a new group of retailers entered. In 1995 French retailers Leclerc, Auchan, and Docks de France opened stores and were followed in 1996 by Casino. Jeronimo Martins, from Portugal, entered joint ventures to operate a chain of local discount food stores and a cash and carry chain in 1995 and also develop Jumbo hypermarkets themselves. In the same year Tesco purchased a chain of small supermarkets to effect their entry into the market. Most importantly, perhaps, Metro and Tengelman entered initially with their discount formats of Tip and Plus in September 1995. In some cases changes in the ownership of the holding companies, for example Docks de France and Auchan, have slowed developments of this group of retailers but in many cases expansion has been rapid and substantial. Metro, for example, has increased the number of its discount stores [37 Tip stores in 1997] and has also introduced its hypermarket format REAL [4 opened in 1997 and 4 planned for 1998], DIY stores [1 Praktiker store opened in 1997], Vobis computer stores and Adler clothing stores with plans to introduce a sporting goods chain well advanced by 1998.

Phase 3: Consolidation. By 1997 the signs of consolidation are starting to be apparent. Jeronimo Martins' entry in 1995 involved joint ventures with a Polish company and Booker the UK wholesaler. These interests were bought out in 1997 and 1998 by Jeronimo Martins and the operations [243 Biedronka discount stores and 68 cash and carry depots at the end 1997] are now wholly-owned together with the two Jumbo hypermarkets. Interkontakt, the Czech company, has purchased the last substantial chain of state stores [PHS] to give it a network of over 550 stores. The joint venture between Ahold and Allkauf which operated hypermarkets, supermarkets and discount stores has broken up. Billa has sold its operation to Rewe. The purchase of Makro by Metro further consolidates the ownership structure of large sales units particularly with the sale of Metro's discount operation to Jeronimo Martins in late 1998. Within this current phase, however, there are still new entrants, notably in the non-food sector, which are increasing the competition.

The three phases are indicative of stages in an overall process. The phases do not have clear-cut start and end dates but merge into each other. It must also be appreciated that firms may be leaders or laggards in the overall process of internationalisation of retailing and whilst the market may have moved forward laggard firms may culturally still be in an earlier phase. The move into new phases in the market is an additive process, not a process of substitution. Thus whilst some firms are involved in consolidation others are entering Poland for the first time and are pioneering. Given the dynamics of the market in Poland phase 3 is not the end of the process. Further stages in the process will occur.

THE HYPERMARKET SECTOR

At the end of 1996 there were 9 foreign-owned hypermarkets,[2] by the end of 1997 there were 21 plus 13 Makro units which operated, in effect, as hypermarkets. The 34 units were operated by 10 different international retail companies in Poland. A further 30 stores were announced to be opened by the end of 1998. Table 4 shows the position in the autumn of 1998 with 43 stores in operation. In addition, there were seven Polish-owned hypermarkets operating at the end of the first quarter of 1998. Foreign investors clearly dominate the hypermarket sector owning over 80% of stores and an even larger share of total retail space since foreign-owned hypermarkets tend to be larger than domestically-owned stores. Furthermore, the land acquisition programme of the foreign retailers is such that they will dominate the opening programme of hypermarkets for several years. The logistic curve of increase in hypermarket number and sales space is well established from evidence in Western Europe (Dawson 1984). The current position in Poland would suggest that 1997 represents the turning point before rapid expansion with increasing annual rates of increase.

In terms of ownership structure, there are no examples of foreign/ domestic joint ventures operating in the sector. The preferred ownership structure is 100% foreign-owned. This makes retailing somewhat different from many other sectors (Neimans 1993; Nasierowski 1996;

TABLE 4. Foreign-Owned Hypermarkets Operating in Autumn 1998

Fascia [Owner]	Year of market entry for hypermarkets	Number of units	Estimated sales in 1997 [mil Euro]
Hit [Dohle Handelsgruppe[1]]	1994	6	223
Makro [Mekro[1]]	1994	14	1528[5]
Leclerc[2]	1995	3	24
Jumbo [Jeronimo Martins[3]]	1996	2	
Auchan[2]	1996	3	48
Géant [Casino,Promodès[2]]	1996	3	127
Real [Metro[1]]	1997	6	. . .[5]
Carrefour[2]	1997	3	
Allkauf [Ahold[4]]	1997	2	
Selgros [REWE, Otto Versand[1]]	1997	1	

Notes:
1 Owner based in Germany
2 Owner based in France
3 Owner based in Portugal
4 Owner based in Netherlands
5 Total sales of Metro including Real and other formats

Sources: Retail Newsletter 1998, Eveno 1998a, 1998b, M+M Eurodata, Company interviews

Ali and Mirza 1997). There is one example of a joint venture involving two German companies, though strictly speaking it is a mixed cash and carry and hypermarket format. The Polish store is owned and managed by the German-registered joint venture Selgros which is jointly owned by Rewe and Otto Versand. One of the two cases of a joint venture between two foreign-owned firms specifically to operate hypermarkets in Poland collapsed when Metro bought out the parent Allkauf from under Ahold. Ahold subsequently negotiated the purchase of the Metro portion of the development, making the stores totally owned by Ahold.

All foreign-owned hypermarket operators interviewed during the research had ambitious expansion plans, which if it is assumed that all existing land holdings are developed, imply around 100 or more hypermarkets in operation by 2000 and a capital commitment of around $2-3 bn. This will undoubtedly be a significant capital investment but the development of banked land may not proceed quite as smoothly, or as quickly, as in-country directors would wish. Even if stores are opened according to plan, Poland has 93 cities and towns with a population greater than 50,000 people so the coverage of hypermarkets, even at 100 stores, will still be quite sparse by West European standards.

Currently the most favoured (and fought over) locations are the major conurbations of Warsaw, Katowice, Krakow, Wielkopolska, Szczecin, Gdansk/Gdynia and Lodz. In these cities, massive housing areas often at the end of tram lines continue to provide opportunities for hypermarket development provided consumer demand for the format continues to grow. Obtaining suitable locations within these cities poses a variety of problems including overcoming historic bureaucratic tendencies (Niznik and Riley 1994). The struggle to establish the single 'shut out' store in medium-sized cities and towns is an interesting strategic challenge: is the correct format for this market a scaled-down hypermarket with a large non-food section or a large supermarket that concentrates principally on food lines and household goods?

Is Hypermarket Competition Real?

While the low density of hypermarkets operating in Poland suggests that there is unlikely to be real competition between stores for at least the next three years, the main reason for the lack of head-to-head competition has more to do with the operational problems that dominate management concerns. Nonetheless, in Warsaw and soon Kato-wice and Poznan consumers with cars will have some choice of hyper-markets. In general, West European retailing formats of parent companies are being introduced for lack of alternatives, *but*, long-term success depends on adapting to Polish consumer tastes, buying habits and spending patterns. The lack of responsiveness to Polish tastes is reflected in the choice of assortments: a tendency to follow the pio-neers and then adjust to the local situation thereafter. Tailoring of assortments seems to be following a relatively expensive pattern of trial-and-error. Many store managers have been surprised by the strength and variety of regional tastes and continuing consumer loyal-ty to national and regional brands.

In-store merchandising in the hypermarkets is similarly dynamic and at times apparently unfocused. There does seem to be a clear trend towards reducing the assortment range driven by expatriate heads of buying. Polish managers were sometimes criticised for pre-ferring breadth of range over focus and consistent availability. As yet there is no obvious Polish style of merchandising: German-owned hypermarkets look like their parent stores in Germany and contrast sharply with French-owned hypermarkets which look very similar to those operated by the parents in France. This is reflected in in-store displays and promotions: some favouring low density, others high density of shelf barkers and display materials. Control of local mark-downs is currently centralised, probably reflecting uncertainty and lack of trust in the judgment of inexperienced Polish store managers operating within the parameters of store stock control and pricing systems.

Much is made of the curiosity and desire for novelty of Polish consumers and the widespread need for providing more information points, demonstrations and tastings than would be the case in West-ern Europe. The accent in customer service is thus on educating consumers rather than dealing with product returns and complaints. Market research on customers is currently limited by the lack of national coverage of store networks and of reliable EPOS data. Sur-vey research in the current project confirmed that Polish customers are (unsurprisingly) unfamiliar with the new retailing formats being introduced by international retailers but so far there is strong interest in the offer and a positive response to the novelty of an expanded choice of product. However, the Polish consumer is an inveterate experimenter.

Staff development and performance monitoring are widely recognised as major constraints on the development of national store networks. Recruitment of well-educated and motivated management trainees is not generally a problem, the much greater difficulty is retaining trained and disciplined junior and middle-level managers. For example, many graduate trainees complain of the unsocial working hours required of store managers. Perhaps the most fundamental constraint on building a management cadre to operate a national store network is the lack of geographical mobility caused by the underdeveloped state of the middle-income housing market.[3]

A key challenge for store management is creating a service-oriented retail culture when operational systems are not yet reliable. The pre-1989 tradition of stock-outs and rationing still haunts efforts to create a culture of customer care and education. This uncertainty is a direct consequence of the underdeveloped state of logistics and supply chain management systems in Poland. Shrinkage also remains a major problem both at the front of the store and at the back. No one seems to have a clear view of how sensitive the Polish consumer is to obtrusive security measures. Security staff are evident in all stores but their effectiveness is largely unmeasured.

The more difficult challenge is fighting shrinkage by store staff. There persists an uneasy trade-off between the 'iron fist' traditions of pre-1989 when staff were automatically surcharged for any stock losses, and building a trusted and self-disciplined retail team. Until logistics systems are improved and store deliveries are reduced to a manageable frequency, shrinkage from the 'backdoor' will remain a problem. Stock management in-store is often very difficult: some stores receive up to 150 deliveries per day from any of 500 different suppliers. Since national store networks are still being created, regional distribution centres have not yet been built, which necessitates the use of in-store warehousing. Unsurprisingly significant ramp losses do occur. Store maintenance and house keeping provide further problems for store managers. While most stores have new equipment, it is rarely state-of-the-art and there are teething problems in teaching staff how to use it correctly. After-sales service of equipment is still unreliable.

STRATEGIC IMPLICATIONS
OF HYPERMARKET DEVELOPMENT

There are a number of potential and currently real implications associated with the further development of hypermarket networks in Poland:

- Intra-type competition between hypermarkets is some way off. Everyone is pre-occupied with making operating systems work under Polish conditions. The few Polish-owned hypermarkets will therefore have a relatively easy competitive ride over the next few years. The difficulty for such firms is one of market entry rather than competition with Western retailers having access to more capital for site acquisition than have the Polish companies.
- Leveraging scale benefits in buying is difficult given current in-store management systems and supply chains. These scale benefits are the core of hypermarket profitability in Western Europe. Changes are needed in in-store management systems in order to satisfy consumer preferences and improve store productivity and solutions to supply chain problems are needed before leverage of scale benefits is possible.
- The impact of hypermarkets on supply chains of Polish food manufacturers and processors and also ultimately on the primary productive sector are likely to be dramatic over the next few years (Peng and Heath 1996). There is already evidence that Western retailers are competing with each other to secure contracts with the more forward-looking Polish suppliers.
- Supply chain constraints result in a relatively large area of high-cost store space being used for in-store warehousing. With the development of store networks central distribution will become feasible and space will be released in the stores for additional sales area. Future store development, particularly in the middle market cities, may result in smaller store sizes supported by central distribution.
- Operational uncertainties and the relative inexperience of ex-patriate and Polish management in dealing with changing conditions means that the parent's domestic profit formula does not apply under Polish conditions. Driving up productivity to parent company standards will have to come later. The implication of

this is that local small shopkeepers whilst initially affected by the new store will not feel the full force of this competition until later when the western retailers seek to increase productivity.

- Logistics systems are gradually emerging to service the hyper-markets but these systems are presently expensive and often op-erated by non-Polish firms. The underdeveloped nature of logis-tics is presently providing opportunities for Polish owner-drivers of vehicles who work on contract to the Western retailers.
- The capital budgeting committee of parent companies is liable to become sceptical about the merits of Polish investment if the par-ent company's financial reserves and overall profitability de-cline. Those that have made the commitment to Poland are un-likely to exit the market solely because of the poor profit performance of Polish investments, at least in the medium term.
- First mover advantages are considerable. The scarcity of a con-sumer culture results in the first store in a community having a high curiosity value and the opportunity to establish quickly a substantial market share. Real estate values then tend to escalate, adding a further cost burden on later entrants.

It is apparent that becoming competitive on costs means progress-ing beyond being merely an importer of a retailing business system from the parent company, to molding and adapting those systems to the Polish context. The priority of firms at the state of development shown in 1998, however, is to establish a network of stores as quickly as possible (Eveno 1998b) and to operate these to basic standards of competence. Establishing a market presence is, at this juncture, of much greater strategic importance than developing advanced market-ing and other systems.

The hypermarket concept is radically new to consumers and suppliers in Poland. The rapid growth of this store format by non-Polish companies is generating rapid change in consumer and company behaviours. West European retailers dominate the hypermarket sector in Poland and this is likely to continue for some years. The hypermarket is only one of several new food formats, including hard-discount stores, supermarkets and con-venience stores, being introduced simultaneously into the Polish market by West European retailers. The hypermarket because of its market power poses the largest strategic challenges to domestic and foreign-based par-ticipants in Polish retailing and its supply base.

NOTES

1. Copies of more extensive papers considering several formats are available on request from the authors. Dawson and Henley 1998a, 1999a, 1999b.
2. The distinction between a hypermarket and a large supermarket is arbitrary. This paper uses the definition that a hypermarket is a store which has a sales area of more than 3,500 m2 selling food and other non-food products.
3. While pubic housing is gradually being privatised, existing tenants have 'grandfather' rights to the property and it is proving difficult to create a market for middle-income housing. Forty-five years of population immobility under communism has also fostered a family system of inter-generational dependency that is highly resistant to geographical mobility.

REFERENCES

Ali, S and Mirza, H (1997) Market-entry strategies in Poland. *Journal of East-West Business*, 3(1), 43-62.

Bauer, A and Carman, J M (1996) Toward explaining differences in the transition of distribution sectors in Central European Economies. *Proc. of Conference of European Marketing Academy.*

Chojnicki, Z, Cryz, T and Parysek J J (1999) Transformations and dilemmas of the Polish economy. In F W Carter and W Maik (editors) Shock-shift in an enlarged Europe. Ashgate, Aldershot, 7-26.

Corporate Assistance (1997) *Strategic Report on Distribution of FMCG in Poland.* Corporate Assistance Warsaw.

Corporate Assistance (1998) *Strategic Report on Distribution of FMCG in Poland.* Corporate Assistance Warsaw.

Corporate Intelligence (1995) *Retailing in Europe: Eastern Europe.* Corporate Intelligence on Retailing, London.

Dawson J A (1984) Structural-spatial relationships in the spread of hypermarket retailing. In: E Kaynak and R Savitt (editors), *Comparative Marketing Systems*, Praeger, New York, 156-182.

Dawson, J A and Henley, J S (1998) Internationalisation of Retailing in Poland: A provisional Assessment. Paper given to Annual Conference of Development Studies Association, Bradford, September.

Dawson, J A and Henley, J S (1999a) The internationalisation of food retailing in Poland: The management of scarcity? *University of Edinburgh Management School, Working Paper* 99/1.

Dawson, J A and Henley, J (1999b) Recent developments and opportunities in Retailing in Poland. *Distribucion y Consumo*, in press.

Dawson, J A and Burt, S (1998) The dynamics of retailing in Europe. In D Pinder (editor) *The New Europe.* Wiley, Chichester.

Domanski, T (1996) (editor) *Nowe Formy Dystrybucji w Polsce.* University of Lodz, Lodz.

EUROSTAT (1998a) *Retailing in the European Economic Area 1997.* Eurostat, Luxembourg.

EUROSTAT (1998b) *Retailing in the Central European Countries 1997.* Eurostat, Luxembourg.

Eveno, R (1998a) Pologne: le match franco-allemand. *Libre Service Actualite,* 16 Avril, 20-23.

Eveno, R (1998b) Tir groupé de Français en Pologne. *Libre Service Actualite,* 5 Novembrc, 25.

Institute of Home Market and Consumption (1997) *Poland's domestic trade in 1996.* Ministry of Economy Warsaw.

Johnson S and Loveman G W (1995) *Starting over in Eastern Europe.* Harvard Business School Press, Cambridge, Mass.

Martin, P (1997) *Retailing in Central and Eastern Europe.* FT Publishing, London.

Nasierowski, W (1996) Emerging patterns of reformation in Central Europe. *Journal of East-West Business,* 2 (1/2), 143-172.

Neimans, J (1993) Market entry approaches for Central Europe. *Journal of Business Strategy,* 14, 2.

Niznik A M and Riley R (1994) Retailing and urban managerialism: process and patterns in Lodz, Poland. *Geographia Polonica,* 63, 25-36.

Peng M W and Heath P S (1996) The growth of the firm in planned economies in transition: Institutions, organization and strategic choice. *Academy of Management Review,* 21, 492-528.

Pütz R (1997) New business formation, privatisation and internationalisation. Aspects of the transformation of Polish retail trade. *Die Erde,* 128, 235-249.

Pütz R (1998a) Polen im transformatoinprozess. Wirtschaftsräumliche disparitäten beim übergang vom plan zum markt. *Geographische Rundschau,* 50(1), 4-12.

Pütz R (1998b) *Einkelhandel im transformatioonsprozess.* L.I.S, Passau.

Retail News Letter (1998) Poland: Foreign retail presence accelerating. *CIES Retail News Letter,* 462, 9.

Seitz, H (1992) Retailing in Eastern Europe: an overview, *International Journal of Retail and Distribution Management,* 20(6), 4-10.

SUBMITTED: 03/99
FIRST REVISION: 05/99
SECOND REVISION: 06/99
ACCEPTED: 07/99

Eastern and Central Europe:
The Impact of the Cultural Environment
on Privatization and Entry Strategies

Peter Geib
Lucie Pfaff

SUMMARY. The aim of this research is to help explain the impact of cultural variables on privatization and market entry strategies in several of the transition economies of Central Europe. The geographic area focus is on the former East Germany, Hungary, Poland, and the Czech Republic. The cultural legacy of communism involves the need to fundamentally change core values. Democratic capitalism requires a cultural re-orientation. The authors seek to examine the implications of cultural impediments and opportunities and to show how successful strategic management seeks to function in a dramatic value transition. Finally, the analysis underlines how each country as well as individual management teams have made progress under the new circumstances. *[Article copies available for a fee from The Haworth Document Delivery Service: 1-800-342-9678. E-mail address: getinfo@haworthpressinc.com <Website: http://www.haworthpressinc.com>]*

KEYWORDS. Transition economies, Central Europe, Czech Republic, Hungary, Poland, privatization, entry strategies

Peter Geib is Professor of Management and Director of International Business at Moorhead State University, Moorhead, MN 56563.

Lucie Pfaff is Professor of Business/Economics and Coordinator of the international Business Program at the College of Mount St. Vincent, Riverdale, NY 10471.

[Haworth co-indexing entry note]: "Eastern and Central Europe: The Impact of the Cultural Environment on Privatization and Entry Strategies." Geib, Peter, and Lucie Pfaff. Co-published simultaneously in *Journal of East-West Business* (International Business Press, an imprint of The Haworth Press, Inc.) Vol. 5, No. 4, 1999, pp. 53-67; and: *Strategic Management in Central and Eastern Europe* (ed: Peter Geib, and Lucie Pfaff) International Business Press, an imprint of The Haworth Press, Inc., 2000, pp. 53-67. Single or multiple copies of this article are available for a fee from The Haworth Document Delivery Service [1-800-342-9678, 9:00 a.m. - 5:00 p.m. (EST). E-mail address: getinfo@haworthpressinc.com].

INTRODUCTION

The Cultural Legacy of Central Planning

After decades under rigid Communist control, the East and Central European countries are in the midst of slow, painful, traumatic changes on their way to market economies. Centralized socialistic planning has left these countries ill-prepared for the transition to a market economy. The whole political, social, and business environments have to be transformed. The aim of this paper is to examine how cultural variables impact privatization and affect various market entry strategies in Poland, The Czech Republic, Hungary, and Germany. The focus is on changing values and how to function in this transition in terms of workable forms of direct investment.

New sets of values have to replace the old ones which were superimposed on several generations by the old regime. Under Marxist theory, only work produced by labor created value. It was the single legitimate source of income, specifically work done in the framework of an enterprise or organization in the public sector (Kornai, 1990). Furthermore, in the party doctrine of centralism, all major government and economic decisions were made by party members at the top. The result was that a few people in high positions made most of the significant decisions and lower and local initiative was practically nonexistent (Harris & Moran, 1992).

Almost everybody of working age in East and Central European countries has spent a life in a job which demanded little except casual obedience. In the new environment, to expect these workers and lower-level managers to make individual decisions, to participate with initiative and imagination, and to take risk is asking for miracles. What is needed is cultural reconditioning. It is difficult to break old habits and such reconditioning will take time. Most likely it will be a generation before the majority of these populations can truly adjust to the culture of a market economy. In terms of entry strategies, it is a question of how best to work with and how best to help re-shape core values in transition economies.

It is the purpose here to examine how cultural conditioning impacts on privatization and entry strategies. Below, some of the different approaches to privatization will be described. It will be shown that the existing cultural mindset is just as much an obstacle in the transformation process as is the absence or poor development of economic institutions.

Methodological Notes

The core of this research is based on data collection and interviews conducted by both authors between 1990-1996. The authors conducted more than 90 on-site interviews over five years with managers in U.S. firms and joint ventures as well as focused research in Germany regarding the privatization process. Many of these interviewed managers were Central Europeans. Besides the direct, on-site research, the authors have examined secondary sources such as government publications and academic literature focusing on the Central European transition. (Sample questions of the structured interviews are in the Appendix.)

Analysis of the Cultural Context

One of the first and best frameworks for analyzing the impact of cultural variables on business activities is Vern Terpstra's model. Part of its great significance lies in his pioneering effort to broaden our understanding of the cultural context by emphasizing political, legal, religious, and ethnic factors on business success or failure. It is more clear than ever that these factors help determine destiny in the global economy. Terpstra's model also provides us with points of departure for operationalizing these factors. Examples of these influences in our research include the importance of ethnicity as the cultural context of the unique German success with privatization and the importance of the Czech historical memory of success with core capitalist values like risk and profit between the great World Wars (Terpstra, 1978).

In the case of most of the transition economies examined here, an emphasis on changing political culture and core social values is clearly relevant. In each case there is a rapid political change from authoritarian political culture to distinctly pluralistic democratic systems. This change has been accompanied by modern legal codes emphasizing due process and property rights under various privatization schemes. This in turn distinctly affects the choice of strategic market entry strategies.

Another example of changing cultural context is the changing system of work-related social values. While the social context still emphasizes a collective group orientation, it increasingly focuses on social and market-oriented values of individuality, risk, material enterprise, and profit. These are also reflected in Terpstra's model. Almost all the interviewees from Central Europe more or less referred to these issues as key to the success of market entry and privatization. One example from Poland is indicative. When managers hire they frequently confront individuals who have long worked in the old system and demand the same level of comprehensive benefits provided by the communist state. These demands under the new system are negotiable and will frequently not be met (On-site interviews, Central Europe, 1990-1996).

A major set of values that has represented an obstacle to development has been the communist brand of isolation and economic protectionism. Central European firms were inefficient and non-competitive since there were no competitive pressures partially due to the ready-made markets within the Soviet empire. This course was a formula for stagnation. These countries have generally made a rapid turnaround and value reorientation based on a consensus to move forward as quickly as possible to a fully functioning market structure with the goal to eventually join the European Union (On-site interviews, Central Europe, 1990-1995). Most striking for the turnaround in each country was the development of an active and dynamic entrepreneurial culture.

Obstacles to Privatization

Privatization should be understood as a transfer of real assets from the state to the private sector. This transfer should be accompanied by a radical reallocation of available productive resources and by restructuring of the existing institutional framework in which production takes place. A new set of core values is required. It will be necessary to introduce new methods of corporate governance with little or no political interference. If privatization is applied this way, it will lead to far-reaching economic and social transformation. However, given the conditions of most post-communist societies, what we observe is often a mere transfer of title without the necessary structural changes (Frydman, 1993).

From the outset, privatization has seen considerable success in the small business sector. The privatized shops and service outlets are usually owner-managed and have low capital requirements. In the simple structure of the sole proprietorship, success depends on the entrepreneurial skills of the owner-manager.

The privatization of large industries encounters serious technical and political obstacles. For instance, the existing management has little interest in giving up jobs and positions, but instead has in many cases forced the state to relinquish some of its property rights in management's favor. Where mass giveaways have been proposed, enterprise managers, as well as workers, have objected to the process. In Poland, e.g., opponents of mass privatization have been able to block legislation aimed at mass distribution (Frydman, 1993) and postpone its implementation by several years (Duvivier, 1997).

Policies initiated failed to take into consideration a number of constraints which are due to the communist legacy: a highly concentrated and outmoded industrial structure, lack of financial infrastructure and sound banking system, as well as the absence of a functional legal code. Banks in every Central European system have been an obstacle to change because of the economic values they embody. In the old system, banks essentially perform one function–channeling money from government to state-owned enterprises. Clearly banks must be completely modernized to perform multifaceted roles in market economies as, for instance, to perform risk assessment of borrowers which was absent in the state enterprise system. Furthermore, the principles and values associated with secure private ownership, private property, and an understanding of how markets work are lacking. What is often overlooked is the distorted behavior patterns of managers, workers, and consumers which will affect every aspect of economic performance (Portes, 1993).

It is not surprising that workers are more interested in maintaining employment than in maximizing profits. Wages are more important than dividends. Managers in uncompetitive enterprises want to maintain the status quo and hope that state subsidies will continue (Frydman, 1993). Even in Germany, with rapid privatization and tremendous subsidization by the Bonn government, investors still have to deal with the work and investment mentality inherited from the socialistic state. The East German workforce has proved to be unproductive by western standards and in need of massive relocation and retraining (Henzler, 1992; Woodruff, 1998).

DIFFERENT PATHS TO PRIVATIZATION

Under the former regimes, the people of the region had always been told the state's assets belonged to them. They expected to be beneficiaries of the distribution of state assets (Lieberman, 1997). This made it necessary to define methods of general participation in the transfer. In each case, some form of voucher system was used to achieve large-scale participation. Individual countries have adopted different institutional arrangements for mass privatization. These arrangements depended on the willingness of government to proceed with speedy privatization, or, even if government was willing, other stakeholders were able to retard the process (Nestor, 1997).

Whatever the prescription, the main question remains, how to create capitalism without first creating capitalists. In western economies, the existence of a capital-owning class will assist in the mobilization of capital either through borrowing or through asset sale to stimulate the economy in a downturn. Here, however, there is no such class and the asset value of state enterprises is severely depressed and therefore it is difficult for the post-communist state to sell assets to generate cash for investment or to stimulate demand (Parker, 1993). As a result, the state of affairs in these countries has been difficult and not until the 1994-1995 period can some improvement be observed.

Hungary

Because of the reluctance of management and the workforce to give up many rights, only a small portion of the large enterprises are privately owned. Most large firms are in a system of institutional cross-ownership, with companies which are still largely state-held, and banks holding stakes in each other. Due to this web of institutional cross-ownership and special arrangement, ownership rights are not clearly defined and neither party, state, nor management can effectively claim ownership or control. Overall, enterprise managers have dominated the transfer process (Frydman, 1993). The result is that attempts at privatization have produced much smaller numbers than in Poland or the Czech Republic. Initially, in 1990, Kornai describes the situation as ". . . tiny isles of private sector are surrounded by an ocean of state-owned firms" (p. 59). In Hungary, it has been difficult to make strong decisions in favor of privatization because of the political and economic culture of gradualism.

In the meantime, however, privatization legislation has been adopted and an independent state agency, the APVRT, has been formed. This agency has separate supervisory and executive bodies which have considerable autonomy in the planning of their operational method and privatization policy. The setup bears comparison to the German Treuhandanstalt in structure and autonomy. Decision-making is relatively concentrated and the predominant policy is that of selling assets rather than distributing them (Nestor, 1997).

Poland

Poland did not adopt mass privatization as the main method for privatizing its state-owned enterprises. Mass privatization was not an essential element of the initial economic program developed in 1989. It was viewed as one of several methods of a multitrack transformation program (Duvivier, 1997).

The unique situation in Poland included a relatively large number of private businesses and a predominantly private agricultural sector, and its tradition of strong trade unions and workers councils influencing operations of state-owned enterprises. Though nominally owned by the state, during the 1980s state-owned companies resembled more a model of group ownership. This factor strongly influenced the shape and development of privatization (Lewandowski, 1997). All through the period when the Polish Parliament worked on the privatization law, there was pressure from trade unions and workers councils for insider privatization.

Lack of understanding of the process by the public, limited support for mass privatization, and the social and political environment created enough obstacles to delay distribution of shares to the public. The Law on the Privatization of State-Owned Enterprises, passed in 1990, was reworked in early 1993, rejected again, but finally found approval and became effective in June 1993. It provided for two types of enterprises–400 to serve as the base for issue of universal certificates, available to all citizens, and 200 for the issue of compensation share certificates, available for certain pensioners and state employees (Lewandowski, 1997).

Political uncertainties and changes in government delayed the implementation further. Poland's program, also called the National Investment Funds Program, was finally operational in late 1995 (Duvivier, 1997). The law provided for prequalified and selected investment funds to bid for enterprise shares. These funds represented intermediate ownership between citizens and the newly privatized companies (Lieberman, 1997). The distribution of shares attracted a considerable attention and a growing number of investors. By November 1996 more than 24 million Poles (95 percent of the adult population) participated in mass privatization (Lewandowski, 1997).

Poland created a line ministry to oversee privatization. Such an agency is part of the government with no independent legal status and little financial autonomy. Any decision on privatization could be vetoed by both the ministry and state-owned enterprises and this may have directly contributed to the slow process and continuous delay of implementation (Nestor, 1997).

The Czech Republic

The Czech Republic has gone the voucher route from the beginning. In 1991 the Large-Scale Privatization Law was passed. The law featured centralized administration of the program, with institutional control concentrated in the Privatization Ministry and the autonomous National Property Fund. The program planned for early and widespread public involvement, avoidance of preferences for insiders, and only a limited role for management-employee buyout schemes, as well as only limited foreign participation (Desai & Plockova, 1997). The vouchers could be used to bid for shares of a privatized enterprise or for deposit in an "investment fund."

Each enterprise and other interested parties could propose a privatization project and the method of disposition of shares. No firm was required to sell shares for vouchers. Vouchers were used alongside several other privatization methods such as direct acquisition, public offerings, auctions, management-employee buyouts, and free transfers (Desai & Plockova, 1997).

Approved privatization projects reserved an average of 62 percent of a company's shares for voucher distribution. Voucher privatization was then carried out in two "waves"–each wave with several rounds of bidding. In the period from 1991-1995, approximately 1800 firms were wholly or partly privatized through vouchers (Desai & Plockova, 1997).

Because of active public participation in the program, the voucher route of mass privatization led to a fast transfer of title. However, because more than 70 percent of voucher recipients deposited their vouchers in investment funds, the outcome was a considerable concentration of ownership in the investment funds (Frydman, 1993).

The transfer through vouchers and shares, although quite successful in the Czech Republic, did not work well in other countries as, e.g., demonstrated by the Polish case. Limited success can be blamed on the different environment, such as lack of demand for shares by the public, opposition by political and social groups, and political pressure by insiders. For such reasons, in several countries the quick transfer of title did not materialize in a timely fashion.

Germany

In this context a short transgression to East Germany is appropriate to examine an example of privatization through property sales handled by an autonomous agency. The sale of state-owned properties was entrusted to the Treuhandanstalt, a government agency specifically created for this purpose. By 1994, the Treuhand had privatized a large portion of the public properties and its success, in spite of all the controversies, set an example east of the border. By 1995, with the majority of the properties sold, the Treuhandanstalt was closed and a successor agency kept overseeing the transfers still in progress.

Although some countries, like Estonia and Hungary, went the agency route (Nestor, 1997), most transition economies could not use the German model because of the need to distribute state-owned assets among its citizens. However, many countries in the region, when forming joint-stock companies, have opted for the German-style dual board of directors system, in which independent directors form a supervisory board and managers form an executive board (Lieberman, 1997).

In East Germany, systematic change came through the extension of long-standing, well-functioning western institutions and administration. Privatization and restructuring were helped by the large number of potential West German investors and entrepreneurs. However, in spite of fast privatization, the transition period will be much longer than anticipated. Outmoded plants had to be torn down and replaced. Overall, production levels fell. Increasing unemployment and less competitive production kept eastern wages below those of the West. Nevertheless, the stable legal and economic framework does attract sizable outside investment. Although most of it comes from western Germany, many EU and OECD countries are well represented among the investors (Geib & Pfaff, 1995).

But even here, under such favorable conditions, investors have to deal with the socialistic culture of the former GDR and some of the same conditions found in neighboring countries to the East: lack of understanding of market forces, some worker apathy or uncompetitive work ethics, and shortage of qualified managers.

ENTRY STRATEGIES
FOR THE CHANGING CULTURAL ENVIRONMENT

Emphasis on Training and Education

Training and education represent an important strategic management tool at the level of the firm and in terms of transforming the cultural context. Core values need to be addressed, strategic management needs to emphasize new values such as risk, competition, individual initiative and creativity, openness to new ideas, and the development of a trade culture. At the level of the firm, the strategy of choice has been to select appropriate individuals and educate them in all respects. One U.S. chief financial officer in a major Polish joint venture stated a typical philosophy when he said that his firm hired young applicants and then trained employees from sophisticated financial analysis to personal hygiene (On-site interviews, Central Europe, 1990-1996). One individual stated that the most difficult problem has been to learn to think for oneself.

Under the Soviet empire, education in management, market economics, finance, and related areas was obviously disallowed. The loss of these opportunities is profoundly and bitterly felt by several generations. The younger generation of managers perceive education and training as from their oppressive past (On-site interviews, Central Europe, 1990-1996). Managers in Central Europe see training as a principal strategic management tool. It is perceived as a means of teaching important new values such as risk, competition, individual initiative and creativity, openness to new ideas, and the development of an export culture (On-site interviews, Central Europe, 1990-1996). Training needs to occur on a variety of levels. The following case reflects these needs.

"VEB Carl Zeiss Jena" faced bankruptcy after the fall of the Wall (before the fall of the Wall it employed 30,000 people). Its optical products were not in demand in the West, the markets of the former

East bloc had dried up, and antiquated production methods were inefficient and costly to replace.

Lothar Spaeth, the former minister president of BadenWuerttemberg, made a deal with the Treuhand. The company would be divided up. Marketable products and 3,000 employees would be taken over by western Carl Zeiss company. The remaining employees and real estate would continue to belong to the eastern Jenoptik (the name eastern Carl Zeiss used for its products sold in the West).

Guaranteeing 10,200 jobs, Spaeth received a loan of DM 3.6 billion from the government to turn around the eastern company. The eastern combine was split up into small- and medium-sized companies based on technical disciplines. Since January 1, 1994 Jenoptik functions as a holding company, uniting production, regional development, and services under one roof. It is employing 16,800 employees, and is expecting it to rise to 19,100 in 1995.

The strategy: modernize facilities, develop new markets and products, look for possible partners; the western management set new corporate and marketing goals: do not *use* anything old or existing–products on the technological edge–become a global player (Orth & Bezjak, 1995).

Strategic Alliances

Almost all managers emphasize that strategic alliances are essential in Central Europe. The cultural context is one of transition toward building of a new political and economic culture. An attitude of openness to collaboration is a proven strategy. Strategic alliances in a risky transition environment provide common goals for the sharing of risk, research and development, marketing expertise, equity, capital, and other resources. Managers in Central Europe emphasize that strategic alliances that have been marked by success include at the very least the following characteristics:

- care and tight focus
- strong and continuous communication
- the development and sharing of expertise regarding cultural, commercial, financial, and political risk
- global strategies
- flexible internal structure
- financial resources (On-site interviews, Central Europe, 1990-1996)

Perhaps the most important need fulfilled by strategic alliances is the provision of expertise by the host country partner and the familiarity with the market environment. The differing cultural contexts as well as the rapid change underlines the importance of intellectual capital. U.S. or western partners usually bring financial capital, as well as cutting-edge technologies.

Another dimension of entering into alliances is the variety of forms that collaboration can take. The movement is in the direction of more flexibility such as co-production and co-development agreements (On-site interviews, Central Europe, 1990-1996).

Relationship Marketing

Above all the variety of cultural norms, the communist legacy, and the rapid change puts an emphasis on relationship marketing. Virtually every manager interviewed emphasized the need to develop long-term trust relationships in order to do effective business (On-site interviews, Central Europe, 1990-1996). Moreover, interview data suggest that Central Europeans traditionally have a "high context" culture that emphasizes the collective over the individual. This traditional approach substantially predates the communist era but was no doubt reinforced by the communists (On-site interviews, Central Europe, 1990-1996).

Niche Marketing

One of the realities of central European markets is the rapidly emerging informal entrepreneurial culture. Small and medium-sized businesses are springing up everywhere. It is consequently impossible to accurately assess these developments in quantitative analytical terms. But on-site observation in cities like Budapest, Warsaw, and Prague show that small and medium-sized businesses are the fastest-growing sector. But it is clear that to work effectively in this market a firm must send a representative to personally examine changing opportunities and take appropriate initiatives in terms of niche marketing (Onsite-interviews, Central Europe, 1990-1996).

Global Marketing

The strategy of global marketing and aiding in the development of an export culture has been an important factor in the success of many of the firms in Central Europe. The communist culture of isolationism and economic protectionism has been a major obstacle to effective economic development. Each interviewee has sought through training, education, re-engineering, and strategic alliances to make his/her firm a global player on whatever terms possible.

CONCLUSION

It is clear that the cultural legacy of central planning is dramatic and long lasting. It will take a generation to overcome the problems of attitudes and entrenched behavior. At the same time, it is clear that the values of democracy and more open markets are taking hold. The Czech Republic is emerging with exceptional strength based on low inflation of 8 percent and a 6.3 percent growth rate. Poland is advancing at a rate of 5.2 percent with a rate of inflation of 22 percent. Hungary is growing at a rate of 3 percent and Germany's unification is clearly successful. Effective Market Entry Strategies are designed to train, educate, and build intellectual capital in an environment of changing core values.

REFERENCES

Desai, R.M. & Plockova, V. (1997). The Czech Republic. *Between State and Market.* Lieberman, I.W., Nestor, S.S., and Desai, R.M., eds. The World Bank, pp. 190-196.

Duvivier, Y. (1997). Poland. *Between State and Market* Lieberman, I.W., Nestor, S.S., and Desai, R.M., eds. The World Bank, pp. 219-222.

Frydman, R. & Rapaczynski, A. (1993, June). Privatization in Eastern Europe: Is the State Withering Away? *Finance and Development,* 10-13.

Geib, P. (1994). Effective Strategic Management and the Central European Transition. Presentation, Minnesota Academy of Science.

Geib, P. & Pfaff, L. (1995). The Central European Transition: Business Obstacles and Opportunities. *Proceedings,* Midwest Marketing Association, pp. 160-165.

Harris, P. & Moran, R. (1991). *Managing Cultural Differences.* (3rd ed.). Gulf Publishing Co.

Henzler, H. (1992, January/February). Managing the Merger: A Strategy for the New Germany. *Harvard Business Review,* 24-30.

Kornai, J. (1990). The *Road to a Free Economy.* W.W. Norton & Co.

Lewandowski, J. (1997). The Political Context of Mass Privatization in Poland. *Between State and Market.* Lieberman, I.W., Nestor, S.S., and Desai, R.M., eds. The World Bank, pp. 35-39.

Lieberman, I.W. (1997). Mass Privatization in Comparative Perspective. *Between*

State and Market. Lieberman, I.W., Nestor, S.S., and Desai, R.M., eds. The World Bank, pp. 1-9.

Miller, K.L. et al. (1994, November 7). Europe: The Push East. *Business Week*, 48-49.

Nestor, S.S. (1997). Institutional Aspects of Mass Privatization: A Comparative Overview. *Between State and Market*. Lieberman, I.W., Nestor, S.S., and Desai, R.M., eds. The World Bank, pp. 19-27.

Orth, M. & Bezjak, R. (1995, February). Jena. *Deutschland*, (1), 22-26.

Parker, R. (1993, Winter). Delusions of "Shock Therapy." *Dissent*, 72-80.

Pond, E. (1993). *Beyond the Wall*. The Brookings Institution.

Portes, R. (Ed.). (1993). *Economic Transformation in Central Europe: A Progress Report*. Center for Economic Policy Research.

Terpstra, V. (1978). *The Cultural Environment of International Business*. Southwest.

The Economist. (1996, Jan. 6-12). Emerging Market Indicators, 90.

Woodruff, D. (1998, July 20). Rising From The Rubble. *Business Week*. 12OE4-12OE6.

Zajicek, E.K. & Heisler, J.B. (1995, Spring). The Economic Transformation of Eastern Europe: The Case of Poland. The *American Economist*, 39, (1), 84-88.

SUBMITTED: 02/99
FIRST REVISION: 03/99
SECOND REVISION: 05/99
ACCEPTED: 06/99

APPENDIX

I. Sample questions of the structured interviews

What is your assessment of the macro-economic changes that have been underway since 1989? How do they relate to the political changes?

What is your assessment of the impact of macro-economic reforms on the strategic management of U.S. firms?

What is your view of the principal strategic management opportunities and problems in U.S. firms?

What is your view of the organizational and corporate culture changes that have to be made for the firm to effectively function in this transition?

What is your view of the monetary system and specific threats and opportunities stemming from it?

What is your view of the banking system and the threats and opportunities stemming from it?

What is your view of the status of intellectual property and the protection provided for it by the evolving legal system in Hungary, Poland, and the Czech Republic?

What is your perception of the threats and opportunities to your business presented by the evolving legal framework?

What are effective criteria for a joint venture?

Are the Central European countries effective bases for exporting?

Banking Systems in Eastern Europe

Alina Zapalska
Georgine Fogel
Dallas Brozik

SUMMARY. This paper offers a study of the development of the commercial banking system in two East European countries. Based on surveys conducted in Hungary and Poland, the authors discuss elements of the competitive market structure in the banking sector. Findings indicate that the commercial banks in Hungary and Poland have become more competitive, but there are differences between the two countries, especially in the way that the banks use sources of foreign funds. *[Article copies available for a fee from The Haworth Document Delivery Service: 1-800-342-9678. E-mail address: getinfo@haworthpressinc.com <Website: http:// www.haworthpressinc.com>]*

KEYWORDS. Banking, financial management, Hungary, Poland, competition, technology adoption, marketing adoption, marketing development

INTRODUCTION

The past decade in Central and Eastern Europe (CEE) has witnessed economic measures to encourage small business development, enter-

Alina Zapalska is Associate Professor of Economics in the Division of Finance and Economics at Marshall University, Huntington, WV 25755-2320.

Georgine Fogel is Associate Professor and Chairperson, Marketing and Management, Management Studies Department, Salem-Teikyo University, Salem, WV 26426.

Dallas Brozik is Associate Professor of Finance in the Division of Finance and Economics at Marshall University, Huntington, WV 25755-2320.

[Haworth co-indexing entry note]: "Banking Systems in Eastern Europe." Zapalska, Alina, Georgine Fogel, and Dallas Brozik. Co-published simultaneously in *Journal of East-West Business* (International Business Press, an imprint of The Haworth Press, Inc.) Vol. 5, No. 4, 1999, pp. 69-85; and: *Strategic Management in Central and Eastern Europe* (ed: Peter Geib, and Lucie Pfaff) International Business Press, an imprint of The Haworth Press, Inc., 2000, pp. 69-85. Single or multiple copies of this article are available for a fee from The Haworth Document Delivery Service [1-800-342-9678, 9:00 a.m. - 5:00 p.m. (EST). E-mail address: getinfo@haworthpressinc.com].

69

prise management, bank and financial reforms, the introduction of income taxation, and the beginning of price and import liberalization. Bank privatization and the establishment of a commercial banking system are a difficult phase in the transition to a market economy. Much has been written about economic reforms in CEE countries, but little attention has been paid to banking issues.

This paper presents the results of surveys on banking competition in two CEE countries, Hungary and Poland. The objective is to describe the nature and level of competition in the banking sector in these two countries. While central banks will indeed affect the structure of the banking community, this paper focuses on how commercial banks operate within their own environment. Considerable progress has been made in establishing an independent commercial banking system since reforms started in the late eighties. The findings reveal that although the structure of the banking system of the two countries is somewhat different, there are signs of competition in the financial markets.

LITERATURE REVIEW

Saunders (et al., 1993) argues that central to a successful transformation in Central and Eastern Europe is a strong and stable banking system in which savers and investors have confidence. Others maintain that it is difficult to imagine any successful transition from a socialist to a capitalist economy without the banking system operating at a reasonable level of efficiency (Thorne, 1993; Steinherr, 1993; Perotti, 1993; Wagner, 1993).

Dittus (1994) shows that bank behavior in the former Czechoslovakia, Hungary, and Poland has changed dramatically since reform started. In 1992, for example, the three countries introduced improved bank regulation and supervision in response to non-performing loans. Dittus states that it is difficult to measure the degree of competition in the banking sector of the post-communist economies. He believes there are many ways to improve the banking systems in CEE countries.

Effective competition in banking can lower the price of financial services or increase the variety and quality of services at a given price. In order to measure competitive forces in the banking sector, Dittus (1994) uses two types of indirect indicators, the concentration of the banking system and access of domestic residents to foreign banking services. His results show that the degree of concentration of both loans and deposits was very high at the beginning of the reforms but has declined since reforms were implemented. The number of foreign banks and joint ventures has also increased in the three countries. This further contributed to creating competitive pressures in the financial markets.

Abel (et al., 1994) argues that the entry of many new banks appears to have improved competition in trade financing and depositing sectors of CEE countries. The market for loans continues to be dominated by few banks with substantial capital base to extend such loans. Dittus (1994) claims that strong competition among domestic banks is caused mainly by individuals and domestic enterprises having access to foreign banking services and instruments denominated in foreign currency. According to Dittus (1994) this change in behavior is linked to the changes in the economic and legal environment that banks are facing now. In this view, banks, like enterprises, react to changed constraints and incentives. This concept has been supported by others (Saunders et al., 1993; Thorne, 1993; Wagner, 1993; Perotti, 1993; Steinherr, 1993; and Shiffman, 1993).

Steinherr (1993) argues that the optimal configuration of financial markets in Eastern Europe is both a theoretical and empirical question. The choice is most likely to be between the broad-based German universal banking model and the narrow-based Japanese model. The Japanese system can sustain high leverage within the banking system and thereby finance rapid growth, which all the East European countries need badly. The German system has the advantages of being better known in Eastern Europe and of being the neighbor's system. The German system is more adaptable to changes in the future and less exposed to the risk of collapse.

The literature review indicates that it is important to support a competitive environment for domestic banks. According to Bonin (et al., 1998), competition in the banking industry can be fostered in many ways. He states that the proliferation of many small, undercapitalized, and inexperienced banks is not a good way to create a competitive environment. A small country can have a competitive financial system even with just a few banks. Competitive practices follow when the capital markets are open and there are no barriers to entry. The ability of customers to take all or part of their banking business abroad and the ability of foreign banks to enter can be combined to make a concentrated small country's banking system highly competitive.

BACKGROUND OF THE BANKING SECTOR IN HUNGARY AND POLAND

Reforms of the Hungarian banking system began on January 1, 1987, when a two-tier banking system was initiated by transforming the National Bank of Hungary (MNB) into a more traditional central bank. MNB is charged with safeguarding the external and internal purchasing power of the forint by utilizing monetary instruments. MNB uses refinancing policy, establishes regulations on mandatory reserves and liquidity reserves, manages the exchange rate policy, influences interest rates, and conducts open market operations. MNB shares oversight of the banking sector with the State Bank Supervision (SBS) established under the Ministry of Finance in 1987. The SBS is responsible for exercising the government's supervision of the banking sector.

The Hungarian banking system has gone through a remarkable transformation since 1987 from money-losing state-owned monoliths to private enterprises and a strong presence of foreign financial institutions. In 1987, there was a total of 115 branches of 15 commercial banks, and by the end of 1997 there were 44 banks with several thousand bank branches, and new branch offices were being opened almost every day.

In 1995 more than half of the banks located in Hungary were of foreign ownership, and by 1997 this increased to 61 percent (State Financial and Capital Control, Hungarian National Bank Annual Report, 1997). Privatization was practically completed by the beginning of 1998. Today, the state has a stake in only three banks (National Savings and Commercial Bank Ltd., Posta Bank and Savings Bank Corporation, and Realbank Co. Ltd.), and the state is no longer a majority owner in these institutions. Foreign institutional investors in the Hungarian banking market include such international companies as ABN-Amro, BNP-Dresdner Bank, CIB, Citibank, Bankers' Trust, and Raiffeisen Unicbank.

Banking services in Hungary have undergone substantial development in recent years. But 70% of the banks' revenues are from interest received and credits granted while only 30% is derived from banking services. By the end of 1996, less than 10 years after the Hungarian Foreign Trade Bank Ltd. issued the first Hungarian bankcard, nearly 1.3 million bankcards were in circulation. Profits in 1996 were double of those in 1994. Table 1 presents the total assets of the five largest banks in Hungary.

Given the high and relatively volatile inflation rate in Hungary, long-term borrowing in forints at fixed interest rates has been difficult. Most lending by commercial banks generally takes the form of a floating interest rate note for periods shorter than one year. In terms of corporate services, Hungarian banks are not eager to lend on a long-term basis. Given the cascade of insolvencies arising from stricter bankruptcy legislation, banks have been risk averse. Taking inflation into consideration, lending activities were essentially static in the mid-1990s. For borrowers, the cost of borrowing is prohibitively high. The current nominal interest rate is close to 20 percent, composed of an annualized inflation rate of 10 percent and a real interest rate of close to 10 percent.

In customer service, foreign-owned banks have a competitive edge over Hungarian banks, but many Hungarian banks have recently developed a variety of retail instruments to attract more clients. ATM machines and credit cards have become widespread and continue to increase in usage. Due to greater foreign presence, the lowering of interest rates, and greater competition, capital has become more readily available on a general basis. The number of foreign banks and

TABLE 1. Share of Five Largest Hungarian Banks in Total Banking Assets

Name of Bank	Assets (HUF Billion)	Percent of Total
National Savings & Commercial Bank	1,249	22.0%
Postabank	387	6.8%
Hungarian Commercial & Credit Bank	367	6.5%
Hungarian Credit Bank	348	6.1%
Hungarian Foreign Trade Bank	348	6.1%
Five Largest Banks	2,699	47.5%
Total Bank Assets	5,678	100%

Source: National Trade Data Bank, Country Commercial Guides, Hungary.

subsidiaries has grown from 21 in 1988 to 62 in 1995. As a result of the switch to the new giro system, interbank money transfers can be conducted in a unified system within 24 hours. Legislation written in 1991 to regulate financial services has been replaced by a new law intended to conform to EU standards. Act CXII of 1996 on Credit Institution and Financial Enterprises came into effect on January 1, 1997. One of the main goals of the new regulations is to protect investors' interests and conform to EU standards.

Until 1988, the Polish banking system was, in effect, a one-tier organization consisting of one central bank. In 1988, the first banking reform took place with the spin-off of the largest Polish retail bank–PKO BP–from the central bank structure. In 1989, a new banking law was introduced, and nine regional commercial banks were established. The shares of the five largest Polish banks in banking assets reported by Miklaszewska (1994) are presented in Table 2.

Poland could develop its financial framework by adapting an existing Western framework. The highly centralized banking system could be broken down to avoid monopolization. Bank restructuring appears to be a prerequisite for increased competition. According to Steinherr (1993), the American model is inappropriate for Poland. The German model is recommended, but it should be weighed against the risk of high concentration. Steinherr states (1993) that it is important to maintain markets that are contestable in the emerging banking structures in Eastern Europe. Rather than relying only on legislative means, it is

TABLE 2. Share of Five Largest Polish Banks in Total Banking Assets

Bank	Assets (Old Zlotys Billion)	Percent of Total
PKO BP	188,042	15%
PKO SA	165,750	14%
BGZ (Cooperative sector)	103,813	9%
Bank Handlowy	87,128	7%
Powszechny Bank Credytowy	1,807	5%
Five Largest Banks	606,540	50%
Total Assets of Commercial Banks	1,209,529	100%

Source: Miklaszewska, 1994.

preferable to retain gates open to foreign bank entries. The Polish banking system is quickly modernizing and is assisted substantially by foreign banks, but recently the Finance Ministry wanted to consolidate the largest Polish banks to enable them to compete against foreign players in Poland. At the same time, efforts are being made to attract foreign capital to the banking industry.

COMPETITION

Economic theory suggests that the market structure of an industry has a major influence on the competitive performance of firms within the industry. The principal elements of structure that are believed to influence behavior include the number of firms, the size distribution of the firms, product differentiation and substitutes, and entry conditions. Many rivals, little concentration, minimal product differentiation, and relatively free entry presumably make intensive rivalry, causing socially beneficial economic results. Few rivals, high concentration, significant product differentiation, and high barriers to entry describe a less competitive and, presumably, inferior market structure. Competition is seen as economically and socially beneficial and is a basic tenet of the free enterprise system. Efficiency is generally associated with competition. Under conditions of perfect competition, profits are maximized at prices and levels of output which bring about an optimum allocation of resources.

In recent years, banking systems in major countries underwent a wave of deregulation, stemming from the necessity to compromise between low price that competition creates and the increased risk and fragility level. One of the main goals of the European Community was to increase competition in European banking through harmonization of regulation, mutual recognition of rules and regulations, and home country control. In the US, there was gradual lifting of restrictions on interstate branching and universal banking. In all major financial markets, competition also increased from non-bank financial intermediaries. The fragility of the financial system may arise independently from competitive structure. It is believed that regulation alone cannot be a remedy but should be aided by appropriate market mechanisms and careful bank examination.

The optimal configuration of financial markets is both a theoretical and an empirical question. Finding the best competitive environment in the banking sector in CEE countries is not simple. Empirical evidence can be found in the market-based systems of the United States and the United Kingdom, as well as the more central-bank-based systems in Germany, other European countries, and Japan. As shown in Table 3, developed economics show surprisingly differentiated structures in their banking systems.

Existing banking systems encompass a wide range of market situations. In some cases, competition is intense; in other cases it is virtually nonexistent. In general, competition in banking is restricted mainly by governmental regulations such as entry modes, requirements for

TABLE 3. Banking System–Selected Data

Country	Number of Commercial Banks	Number of Savings and Mutual Banks	Market Share of Five Largest Institutions
Belgium	85	29	58%
Denmark	78	165	77%
France	404	421	43%
Germany	299	594	26%
Greece	34	0	63%
Hungary	42	2	47%
Ireland	33	2	45%
Italy	267	813	53%
Luxembourg	166	49	26%
Netherlands	89	53	84%
Portugal	29	1	56%
Spain	145	188	39%
United Kingdom	556	163	29%
EEC	2,183	2,478	14%
United States	12,689	3,323	14%
Japan	145	1,080	25%

Sources: Information obtained from individual country's banking associations and central banks and Miklaszewska (1994).

branching, new bank establishments, interest rates on deposits and loans, and portfolio composition management.

The creation of a sound and efficient banking system in CEE countries cannot be accomplished overnight. In a market economy, the banking system is the key institution for providing credit to enterprises and achieving macroeconomic equilibrium. Hungary and Poland introduced many changes in the institutional structure of the banking system and monetary policies with the aim of promoting flexibility and efficiency of financial intermediation. Changes included the separation of central bank functions from those of commercial banks, the refinements of liquidity control for households and enterprises, the incipient formation of markets for financial instruments, and more liberal interest rates. With the establishment of the two-tier banking system, Hungarian and Polish banks have been exposed to competitive pressures.

SURVEY RESULTS

In order to understand competitive forces in the banking sector, surveys were conducted among 44 Hungarian and 81 Polish banks including foreign-owned and joint-venture operations. The objective was to evaluate: (1) how differentiated the banking system is; (2) to what degree banks are exposed to competition; (3) the banks' attitude towards customers and competitors; (4) whether the banks' strategy depends on their ownership structure, size or some other factors; and (5) what are the most important strategic issues perceived by Hungarian and Polish banks. Fifty-two percent (52%) of the banks in Hungary and sixty-nine percent (69%) of the banks in Poland responded.

The distribution of bank services is reported in Table 4.

The majority of bank clients were domestic, and over 40% were individual while about one-third were corporate clients. Services offered to international clients were reported to be 27% in Hungary and 24% in Poland. The similarity of the distribution of the services offered by the banks in both countries indicates that the markets in both countries are quite similar. It should be expected that the banks should exhibit similar operating characteristics if there are no legal impediments to operations.

The distribution of accounts is presented in Table 5. The majority of bank accounts (76% and 89%) was domestic.

TABLE 4. Distribution of Bank Services

Type of Clients	Hungary	Poland
Domestic individual	41%	45%
Domestic corporate	32%	31%
International individual	13%	N/A
International corporate	14%	24%
Total	100%	100%

TABLE 5. Sources of Accounts

Type of Account	Hungary	Poland
Domestic	76%	89%
International	24%	11%

Table 6 presents the sources of capital. According to the table, a substantial share of the sources of bank capital was reported to come from international sources (46% and 33%).

Tables 6 and 7 show that both countries rely most heavily on domestic sources of capital, though Hungary does show a higher exposure to international sources. This could indicate a potential problem for the Hungarian banks. Should the general economy suffer a setback, it is likely that domestic deposits would be repatriated to their home countries. Such a withdrawal would have a greater effect on Hungarian banks and the Hungarian economy. The higher concentration of domestic sources in the Polish banks indicates that they would be better able to withstand an external economic shock.

In terms of banking strategies, the overwhelming majority of banks in both countries reported minimizing risk as a higher priority than maximizing income (Table 7).

This strategy indicates that the banks are concerned with long-term survival over quick profits. Such a strategy is appropriate in developing economies where continued availability of capital is essential for economic growth. It once again appears that the Hungarian banks might be slightly more sensitive to general economic downturns, though there seems to be enough conservatism in the system to prevent an overall meltdown of the financial system.

TABLE 6. Sources of Capital

Source	Hungary	Poland
Domestic	54%	67%
International	46%	33%

TABLE 7. Bank Management Objectives

Objective	Hungary	Poland
Minimize Risk	74%	89%
Maximize Income	26%	11%

The three most often used methods to increase market share position of the bank were exploiting market niches, improving services, and introducing innovation and technology. Few banks reported lowering prices as a method for increasing market share (Table 8).

This focus on products and services is indicative of professional management that recognizes and exploits market opportunities. The similarity of the percentages between the two countries shows that the markets are indeed similar. The lack of price competition implies that the market has yet to develop competitive forces to the extent that would make pricing a critical factor.

The primary reason for introducing product innovation was reported to be long-term strategic goals. Other reasons noted were increasing profits and matching or reacting to competitors (Table 9).

The focus on strategic positioning confirms the professional level of management and the high probability of long-term stability in both countries. The relatively lower percentages given for the other reasons again indicate that neither market has developed a fully competitive structure.

Banks' practices for identifying customer needs included both formal and informal methods (Table 10).

This balanced approach to gathering information concerning the needs and wants of the banks' clients means that there is higher likelihood that the banks will be able to meet those needs as they arise. This is another factor which will promote the stability of the financial industry in both countries.

Most banks reported information by bank staff to be the primary

TABLE 8. Methods Used to Increase Market Position

Method Used	Hungary	Poland
Concentrate on Market Niches	40%	48%
Improve Services	42%	44%
Introduce Innovations/Technology	38%	35%
Lower Prices of Services	10%	3%

TABLE 9. Reasons to Introduce Product Innovations

Reason	Hungary	Poland
Long-Term Strategic Goals	62%	60%
Increase Profits	30%	32%
React to or Match Competitors	26%	12%
Surpass/Outperform Competitors	14%	5%

TABLE 10. Methods for Identifying Customer Needs

Method	Hungary	Poland
Observation/Intuition	32%	39%
Customer Surveys/Research	22%	20%
Secondary Data	18%	14%
Other (experience)	28%	25%

method used for informing customers about new products, and nearly one-third reported to use bank advertisements and promotion (Table 11).

The consistency of management practices is again highlighted by these results. The banks appear to focus on a personal approach to their customers. This could lead to the development of long-term relationships between the banks and their depositors.

The perceived reasons for customer selections of banking services are listed in priority ranking in Table 12. Hungarian banks reported interest rates, quality of services and safety of deposits as the three highest priorities in customer selection of banking. The majority of banks in Poland noted quality of services and interest rates as main reasons for selecting banking services.

It is interesting to note here that Hungarian depositors are relatively

TABLE 11. Methods for Informing Customers About New Products

Method	Hungary	Poland
Information from Bank Staff	38%	41%
Bank Advertisement/Promotion	31%	27%
News/Other Media	19%	17%
Inquiry by Customers	12%	13%

TABLE 12. Perceived Reasons for Customer Selection of Banking Services

Priorities in Selecting Banking Services	Hungary	Poland
Safety of Deposits	22%	5%
Interest Rates	31%	32%
Quality of Services	31%	35%
Past Experience	16%	15%
Service Choices	13%	13%
Location/Proximity	10%	9%
Bank Advertisement	5%	3%

more concerned over the safety of deposits than Polish depositors. This could indicate that Hungarian depositors have less confidence in their banking system and would be more likely to withdraw deposits at the first sign of economic distress. This coupled with the effect of withdrawals from international sources could indicate that the Hungarian banking system could be more vulnerable to changes in economic conditions.

Competition was reported to be taking place in all services as well as selected services. The competitive pressure seems to come mostly for big universal banks. In Hungary 40% of the competition was reported at the national level (Table 13).

These findings indicate that though the competitive nature of the financial markets may not be fully developed, competitive forces are indeed developing. The fact that Hungarian banks experience greater levels of competition from larger, more international banks indicates Hungary's susceptibility to external economic shocks.

The impact of competition was perceived by over half the respondents as likely to change the long-term strategy of the banks (Table 14).

TABLE 13. Perceived Competitive Pressure in the Banking Sector

Area of Competition	Hungary	Poland
All Services	84%	79%
Selected Services	16%	21%
Large, Universal Banks	75%	60%
Small, Specialized Banks	25%	40%
National Level	40%	N/A
Regional Level	26%	15%
Local Level	14%	8%

TABLE 14. Impact of Competition in the Banking Sector

Impact on Bank's Activities	Hungary	Poland
Change Long-Term Strategy	62%	57%
Change Short-Term Strategy	35%	37%
No Impact	3%	6%

Bank management in both countries again demonstrates professional behavior and concern for the long-term survivability of the industry. The relative differences between long-term and short-term strategies provide further evidence of a developing industry that has not yet reached a full competitive structure.

Foreign banks have a more prominent presence in Hungary with 61% of the banks reporting foreign ownership interests. The competitive pressure by foreign banks was perceived to be strong by more than half the respondents in Hungary. In Poland, about one-fifth of the banks reported strong competitive pressure by foreign banks (Table 15).

Hungary's greater reliance on foreign capital is reflected in these figures. As should be expected, if foreign capital is more important in the capital structure, banks will feel more competition from this source. This competition for foreign funds could cause difficulties in an economic downturn.

Approximately half of all respondents believed that competition in the banking sector was equal for all banks (Table 16).

TABLE 15. Perceived Competitive Pressure by Foreign Banks

Competitive Pressure	Hungary	Poland
Strong	52%	21%
Weak	16%	35%
Fair	22%	44%

TABLE 16. Perceived Competitive Environment in the Banking Sector

Impact on Bank's Activities	Hungary	Poland
Equal to All Banks	42%	50%
Unequal to All Banks	33%	50%
No Opinion	15%	0%
No Answer	10%	0%

While most banks do find the competitive nature of the market fair, the fact that a large minority of the banks find competitive forces to be unequal indicates that these financial markets must develop further. There could be vestiges of prior bank regulation and management that are hindering this development, and it would be appropriate for the participants to identify and correct those inhibiting factors.

CONCLUSION

In today's market economy, dynamic features like flexibility and the ability to change and innovate are increasingly important for survival. Competitiveness in commercial banking is unique in that it largely depends on the market environment of the home country. One of the major challenges of CEE countries is the development of a stable, market-oriented financial system.

Hungary and Poland have made many changes in restructuring their banking sectors. The entry of foreign banks has acted as a spur to competition. At the structural level, the number of commercial banks increased to the level that banking services have become somewhat competitive. The primary goal of the banks in the region continues to be minimizing risk, but there are signs of increased competition. Product innovation, the adoption of advanced technologies, a focus on market niche strategies, and improvement of quality standards and customer service operations are becoming part of a long-term strategic orientation that most banks seem to follow.

Competitive forces in Hungary and Poland include a more sophisticated demand for banking services. Customer choices, previous experience, and quality of services have become primary factors in selecting banking preferences among customers. Competition seems to be taking place in all levels of banking activities as well as in specialized services. There is a considerable competitive pressure by big, universal banks and foreign-owned banks/joint ventures. One of the effects of increased competition in the banking sector of the two countries is the increase in product innovation and advanced technology.

The picture that emerges from this survey is one of two banking systems with both similarities and differences. The financial systems of Hungary and Poland appear to have professional managers who focus on the long-term survival of the industry. Both countries evidence financial services industries that are developing but have yet to reach fully competitive levels.

The major difference between the two countries is that Hungary seems to be more dependent on foreign sources of funds, and this is a two-edged sword. If a general economic downturn were to occur, Hungarian banks would likely suffer more than their Polish counterparts. Capital could be withdrawn to its home country thus limiting the funds available to the Hungarian banks. While the Polish banks would be better able to resist this type of external economic shock, during times of prosperity Hungarian banks would have easier access to foreign capital. This could possibly lead to greater economic expansion. The Hungarian banking system seems to be more linked to the world economy while the Polish banking system is more insulated. Time will tell which of these is the better long-term strategy.

REFERENCES

Abel, I. and Bonin, J. (1994). Financial Sector in the Economies in Transition: On the Way to Privatizing Commercial Banks. In J.P. Bonin and Istvan P. Szekely (eds.), *The Development and Reform of Financial Systems in Central and Eastern Europe* pp. 109-126. Edward Elgar: Northampton, MA, USA.

Bonin, J., Mizsei, K., Szekely, I., and Wachtel, P. (1998). *Banking in Transition Economies: Developing Market Oriented Banking Sectors in Eastern Europe.* Edward Elgar: Northampton, MA, USA.

Dittus, P. (1994). Bank Reform in Central Europe. *Journal of Comparative Economics*, *19*, pp. 335-361.

Hungarian National Bank. (1998). *MNB Annual Report*.

International Trade Administration. (1998). *Market Research Reports, Banking Sector*, Washington D.C.

Miklaszewska, E. (1994). Competitive Banking in Central and Eastern Europe. *Working Paper*. Department of Law and Economics. Jagiellonian University, Krakow, Poland.

Ministry of Industry and Commerce, Hungary. (1998). *Annual Report of Statistics*.

National Trade Data Bank, Hungary. (1998). *Country Commercial Guides*.

Perotti, E. (1993). Bank Lending in Transition Economies. *Journal of Banking and Finance*, *17*, pp. 1021-1032.

Saunders, A. and Sommariva, A. (1993). Banking Sector and Restructuring in Eastern Europe. *Journal of Banking and Finance*, *17*, pp. 931-957.

Schiffman, H. (1993). The Role of Banks in Financial Restructuring in Countries of the Former Soviet Union. *Journal of Banking and Finance*, *17*, pp. 1059-1072.

Steinherr, A. (1993). An Innovative Package for Financial Sector Reforms in Eastern European Countries. *Journal of Banking and Finance*, *17*, pp. 1033-1057.

Thorne, A. (1993). Eastern Europe's Experience with Banking Reform: Is There a Role for Banks in the Transition?. *Journal of Banking and Finance*, *17*, pp. 959-1000.

Wagner, H. (1993). Reconstruction of the Financial System in East Germany: Description and Comparison with Eastern Europe. *Journal of Banking and Finance*, *17*, pp. 1001-1019.

SUBMITTED: 03/99
FIRST REVISION: 05/99
SECOND REVISION: 06/99
ACCEPTED: 07/99

Index

APVRT (Hungary), 60

Banking, 69-85
  comparison of countries, 77
  competition in, 75-77
  customer need identification by, 80
  distribution of services, 78
  in Hungary, 3-4,15,72-75,77-83
  impact of competition on, 82
  literature review, 70-72
  management objectives of, 79
  marketing strategies of, 80
  new product information strategies, 81
  perceived competitive pressure, 82, 83
  in Poland, 3-4,72-75,77-83
  in Russia, 26,27
  service selection by, 81
  sources of accounts of, 78
  sources of capital of, 79
  technology adoption by, 80
Bank of Issue (Hungary), 15-16
Belgium, banking system in, 77
Blat (personal favoritism), 30-34
Bribery, in Russia, 30-34
Business education, 16-17,20,60-63
Business transition, in Hungary, 5-21

Central planning, cultural legacy of, 54-55
Colonization, of Polish market, 43-44
Competition
  in Hungarian and Polish banking, 75-77
  in Polish hypermarket retailing, 46-47

Consolidation, of Polish market, 44
Credit insurance, in Hungary, 16
Criminal activity, in Russia, 26
Cultural environment, privatization and, 2,3
Cultural issues
  East-West culture clash in Russia, 23-36
  privatization and, 53-67
Czech Republic, cultural issues and privatization in, 53-67

Data manipulation, in Russia, 29-30
Denmark, banking system in, 77
Deregulation, of banking, 75

East Germany (former), 61-62,71-72, 77
(University of) Edinburgh, 37-52
Education and training, 16-17,20, 62-63
Entrepreneurial motivation, in Hungary, 5-21
Entry strategies, 53-67
Ethical issues
  cross-cultural differences, 29-30
  in Russia, integrative social contracts theory and, 23-36
European Economic Community (EEC), banking system in, 77

Financial management, 69-85
  competition in, 75-77
  in Hungary, 3-4,15-17,72-75,77-83
  literature review, 70-72
  in Poland, 3-4,72-75,77-83
France, banking system in, 77